Improve Your Bridge

Amanda Hawthorn &
Mark Horton

B. T. Batsford, *London*

First published in 1982 by Bibliagora
Revised edition published in 1993 by CollinsWillow
an imprint of HarperCollinsPublishers, London

© Amanda Hawthorn 2000
© Mark Horton 2000

A CIP catalogue record for this book is available from the British Library

ISBN 07134 8569 8

Typeset by Wakewing, High Wycombe
Printed by Creative Print &Design, Ebbw Vale, Wales
for the publishers,
B. T. Batsford, 9 Blenheim Court, Brewery Road,
London N7 9NT

A member of the Chrysalis Group plc

A BATSFORD BRIDGE BOOK
Series Editor: Phil King

Contents

Introduction

To the 1993 Edition

In 1981 I was working closely with the late Rhoda Lederer, running and teaching residential bridge courses up and down the country. We found we were constantly being asked for a book 'for the middle ground'. The people who came to us wanted a book which discussed all the basic bids and plays more thoroughly than could be found in other books for learners – which tended to start by explaining the basics of the game for complete beginners and finish up by discussing quite advanced aspects of competitive bidding and play.

So together we wrote the first edition of this book which was published in 1982 under the title of Improve Your Bridge the Lederer Way as a sequel to Rhoda's highly successful book for beginners, *Learn Bridge with the Lederers*.

Over the last ten years the whole framework of bidding has altered and much of *Improve Your Bridge* – and indeed also of *Learn Bridge with the Lederers* – has become out-moded and incorrect. It was, therefore, impossible to reissue the book without extensive alterations. Sadly, Rhoda Lederer has since died, but I am sure she would heartily approve of the revisions and updating which I have carried out. Chapters have been rewritten and expanded, some with new concepts included. Some material contained in the first edition has been omitted altogether. I have, however, sought to preserve Rhoda's distinctive colloquial style, which her great fan club has found to be easy to understand and follow.

The book is intended for those attending adult education classes or receiving other basic instruction, many of whom intend to play only social bridge or at a local level. I have therefore had to consider carefully how much of modern tournament Acol to incorporate. Moreover, I have deliberately omitted more than a mention of areas such as negative doubles, transfer bidding and two-suited overcalls, to name but a few examples.

I hope that all of you who read this book will find it easy to understand, helpful and, above all, enjoyable. As we all know, bridge is a marvellous game and can be enjoyed no matter what one's standard. However, it is always very satisfactory to do even the basic things more competently and my aim in this latest edition of the book is to aid readers in achieving this objective.

Amanda Hawthorn
November 1993

Introduction to this Edition

If seven days in politics can be a long time – just ask Jeffrey Archer – then seven years in bridge is practically an eternity. The game develops at such a rate that the previous editions of this classic book, which has been out of print for some time, were in need of further revision in a number of areas, particularly in the section dealing with the bidding. Whilst we have concentrated most of our efforts on this important aspect of the game, we have made a number of other changes. Whilst doing so we have endeavoured not to lose the elegant simplicity and charm of the original, for that is what has made the book so popular with teachers and students since the first edition was published in 1982.

Amanda Hawthorn
Mark Horton

PART I
BIDDING

1

One No-Trump Opening Bids – Weak or Strong

All no-trump opening bids, except for a few conventional ones that need not concern us at the moment, are limit bids. That is to say, they tell partner in one bid that the hand is evenly balanced, as well as its upper and lower limits of strength. There are 40 points in the pack, so your fair share is 10 points and on average you won't find yourself holding 15 or more, the minimum for a strong no-trump, more than once or twice in a session of 24 boards. What a pity, therefore, to give up the most preemptive opening one-bid of all, a weak no-trump, which you will pick up time and time again, for the sake of waiting for a strong no-trump hand. Once you do pick up the more-than-your-share of points to open one no-trump, you sit there at the table announcing to all and sundry that you've got the goods, and that the opposition would be ill-advised to try to steal the contract from you.

A point in favour of the strong no-trump is that you are unlikely to come to grief or incur a heavy penalty if you never open One No-Trump with less than 15 points. Your opponents have been warned, and will rarely be in a position to double you for penalties: (remember that the double of any opening one no-trump, whatever its strength, is primarily intended for penalties and not for a take-out).

Turning now to 'weak throughout', that is 12–14 points at all times, you have to face it that occasionally you will get into trouble. One no-trump doubled will usually prove to be costly if your partner is unable to extricate you. However, this does not happen anywhere near often enough to offset the immense pre-emptive value of the weak no-trump opening bid. In any case, worse things have happened at sea than one no-trump doubled, and have you thought of the number of times when your partner turns up with enough points to give you the balance of strength, and you can make the doubled contract?

These exotic moments, though, are not the sole argument in favour of a weak no-trump. Another, which we hope will weigh very heavily with you, is that it is the most pre-emptive of all opening one-bids and, therefore, the most difficult to deal with from the opponents' point of view. You have a minimum of 12 points which leaves 28 for the other three players at the table, and these may well be so divided that no one, including your partner, can speak at all. Time and time again you will find yourself getting away with one no-trump bid and made – even possibly with an overtrick – when the opposition could have made a part-score had they dared to speak. In untutored circles you may get away with it completely, because the opposition don't know how to speak! Suppose, vulnerable, you go down three, undoubled. That's 300 points away – a disaster? Not at all. What you're forgetting is that your opponents must have made nine tricks, that is to say, they scored a no-trump game themselves!

It goes without saying that there are many devices in use to combat a no-trump opening bid, and your brave effort may avail you nothing. But nothing ventured nothing gained, and, on balance, it is our firm belief that you will collect more from using a weak no-trump throughout than you will from insisting on sticking to 'strong' or even 'variable'.

As you progress up the bridge ladder, you will encounter other no-trump ranges. The 'mini' no-trump, based on 10–12 points, still attracts a few aggressive souls, and the medium no-trump, showing 14-16 points is becoming increasingly popular. Both are playable, but remember that as soon as you change the range of this fundamental opening bid, you affect many other areas of your bidding system. The weak no-trump has stood the test of time.

'Prepared' One Club Opening Bid

At one time both one club and one diamond were used as 'convenience' bids, when no sensible rebid presented itself. All too often these bids – particularly one club – are still used, because the player can't be bothered to think of a better bid. This bid has gathered to itself many strange names – fishing club, seeking club, probing club, phoney club. Whatever the name, they all had one thing in common – they demanded a reply, the negative being one diamond. Please understand that this is not the case if you are playing Acol. One club means what it says. It should be taken as a natural club bid unless subsequent bidding reveals otherwise, and it demands no answer. Responder, with nothing to say, should pass. Whatever the name, it leaves the way open for the opposition to come in at a conveniently low level, and gives away bidding space in the essential race to describe the hand.

If you ever, playing Acol, decide to open with a prepared club it must only be if the hand genuinely offers no other possible opening bid, and this will happen only if it doesn't fall into your agreed no-trump range. It will practically never be necessary if you are using a 12–14 point no-trump, because then you will open one no-trump on a balanced hand, and one of a suit if you are unbalanced or have 15 points or more. Nor is it against the law to open one no-trump even when holding a five-card suit (minor or major) if you don't think its good enough to rebid.

(a) ♠ A J 7 2	(b) ♠ A 9 7	(c) ♠ A J 7
♡ K 9 2	♡ Q 9 8 7 2	♡ A Q J 7 2
◇ Q 8 7	◇ Q 8 7	◇ Q 8 7
♣ A 8 5	♣ A 8	♣ 9 8

Hand (a) is a perfect weak no-trump opening, but playing a strong no-trump, you must one club, because if you open one spade you will have to rebid two no-trumps over a response in a minor. If partner responds in a red suit, you must chose between one spade and one no-trump. If he responds one spade, you have an obvious raise to two spades. With hand (b) if you open one heart, you would hardly want to rebid such an anaemic suit, so if the hand comes into your no-trump range, open one no-trump. If you are using a strong no-trump, open one heart, and rebid one no-trump. Note the difference with hand (c). Here your hearts are perfectly rebiddable, so open one heart whatever no-trump you are using

(d) ♠ 7 6 4 2	(e) ♠ 7 6 4 2	(f) ♠ J 8 5 4
♡ A Q 7	♡ A Q 7	♡ J 7 5 3
◇ K 8 6	◇ K Q 5	◇ A K 7
♣ K J 6	♣ K Q 7	♣ A K

On hand (d) you have 13 points, exactly right for a 'weak' no-trump opening bid. It gets the whole hand off your chest, and being a limit bid, you will not have to make a rebid unless partner's response, if any, forces you to take further action. You are not strong enough to open one no-trump if you are using a 'strong' no-trump, and to open one spade would be dangerous with such a weak suit. If you do open one spade and over partner's two of a minor rebid two no-trumps, you might well end up in three no-trumps and lose the first five tricks in spades. Open one club and rebid one no-trump over one diamond or one heart, or raise a spade response to the two level.

Hand (e) has 16 points, and can be opened with one no-trump if you are using 'strong'. It's far too powerful for a one no-trump opening if using 'weak', but this time you can safely open one spade because you have such good outside values. If partner bids another suit at the two-level in response you can safely rebid two no-trumps. If he raises spades you will know you have at least eight spades between you and, as you have no high card points in the suit, it's very likely that that's where the majority your partner's values will be located.

Hand (f) is a splendid one no-trump opening if you are using a 15–17 point range, 'Stayman' giving you all the machinery to find a major suit fit if partner has hearts or spades. If playing a 12–14 point range, it has a satisfactory opening bid of one heart, allowing you to find a major suit fit at once if partner replies in either major, and to rebid two no-trumps over a response of either minor suit.

Transfer Responses to One No-Trump Opening Bids

Transfer bids by responder to both weak and strong no-trump opening bids are now very popular. There is no reason why any partnership should adopt them if they feel that the artificial sequences may lead to bidding misunderstandings, but it is in any event a good idea to understand what the opponents are saying to each other, without having to ask the meaning of each alerted bid (which would be wrong if you have no intention of entering the auction).

The whole purpose of transfer bids is to keep the balanced hand concealed during play, and hope that the opening lead, or subsequent switch, comes into one of its tenaces.

Responder therefore bids the suit just below the one he actually has, and opener is obliged to bid responder's suit himself regardless of his holding in it. All transfer methods retain a bid of two clubs as Stayman to be answered as such. Two diamonds demands a transfer to two hearts and two hearts a transfer to two spades. Responder promises at least five cards in the suit he is demanding opener should bid, and if he then passes when the bidding reverts to him, his hand is a typical weak take-out of an opening one no-trump. If you are wondering how a contract of precisely two diamonds is arrived at, the answer is that it is not!

The bids of two spades and two no-trumps carry different meanings according to what has been agreed between the partnership. Occasionally a route is needed into a minor suit contract and several methods exist. We suggest that you use them both as transfers, two spades showing a club suit, and two no-trumps a diamond suit.

Transfer sequences have a great deal of scope for describing hands which might produce game facing an opening one no-trump bid if the two hands fit well. Here are some examples of hands you might hold when partner opens one no-trump.

(a) ♠ A Q 7 4 2	(b) ♠ A K J 9 8 6	(c) ♠ K Q 7 4
♡ J 8 7	♡ 7 5 3	♡ A Q 9 8 6
◇ Q J 2	◇ K 3	◇ 7 6
♣ J 2	♣ 7 6	♣ 4 3

Hand (a) is much easier to bid using a transfer sequence. Hitherto it was guesswork as to whether to use a weak or a forcing take-out into spades. Now it is bid: 1NT – 2♡ – 2♠ – 2NT showing five spades and 11–12 points. Hand (b) transfers into two spades and can then choose between a bid of three no-trumps or four spades, and hand (c) is bid: 1NT – 2◇ – 2♡ – 2♠ showing five hearts and four spades. The one no-trump opening bidder usually has a good idea of responder's shape and high-card strength and can frequently select the final contract.

When responder holds a stronger hand with the values for game he bids accordingly at his second turn. If you change the hand in our first example to:

♠ A Q 7 4 2
♡ K J 8
◇ Q J 2
♣ J 2

then responder's second bid would be three no-trumps.

A forcing take-out of one no-trump into three of a suit now becomes a slam try showing a powerful single-suited hand.

We have assumed you are playing a weak no-trump, but transfers can be used just as well with any no-trump range.

2

One-Level Opening Bids and Rebids with Unbalanced Hands

When partner hears us open with a bid of one of a suit he will picture either a balanced hand outside the agreed range for a one no-trump opening that will rebid in no-trumps, a hand with at least a five-card suit, or perhaps a 4-4-4-1 hand. A player who opens with one of a suit, and rebids in another suit, is indicating that he would prefer to find a trump fit, and that he does not hold a balanced hand.

Two Five-Card Suits

Hands containing two five-card (and the rare hands of two six-card) suits are easy to bid. Always open with the higher ranked suit except when holding the two black suits. With five clubs and five spades it is generally best to bid one club but, third or fourth in hand when you want to make life difficult for your left-hand opponent to intervene, and when your clubs are rather feeble, a bid of one spade will often work better.

If you think ahead to your rebid you will see the sense behind your choice.

(a) ♠ A Q 8 5 3	(b) ♠ A K 9 5 3	(c) ♠ A K J 8 7
♡ 9	♡ 9	♡ 9 2
◇ K Q 7 5 2	◇ A Q 7 5 2	◇ 10
♣ J 2	♣ A 2	♣ K J 4 3 2

You have two nice biddable suits in hand (a), and let's say that, expecting partner to respond in hearts, you open one diamond. If he obliges with one heart you can say one spade, but now you have conveyed a distinct impression that you hold five diamonds and four spades and partner might put you back to diamonds while all the time he holds three card spade support for you. Worse still, suppose in response to your one diamond, partner bids two clubs. Now think about the message you are passing across the table to your poor unsuspecting partner if you now bid your spades. You have 'reversed' showing longer diamonds than spades and 16+ points. You are forced to rebid two diamonds and now you have concealed a good five-card spade suit, and all because you didn't think before choosing your opening bid.

Try opening one spade instead. If partner responds two hearts, forget about your diamonds and just make a simple rebid of two spades, leaving the rest to your partner. You have bid all that your hand is worth. Of course, if you had an initial response of one no-trump or two clubs, now you would bid naturally, and show your diamonds at the two-level.

Hand (b) contains 17 high-card points, and you may well think it best to open one diamond because, if partner happens to bid two clubs instead of one heart, you are quite strong enough to reverse into two spades. Well, yes, you are, but don't forget that, if you do, partner will always be sure that your diamonds are longer than your spades. So open one spade and, whether partner says two clubs or two hearts, bid three diamonds, which shows just as strong a hand in terms of high card points, but doesn't lie about the distribution.

In hands (a) and (b) we have used the spade and diamond suits but, of course, exactly the same bidding sequences would be correct if we'd used hearts and clubs.

Holding hand (c) open one club if you are first or second to call, and rebid one spade over either red suit. Partner will not be sure whether your shape is 5-4 or 5-5 but if the bidding proceeds further you may get a chance to show the spades again without taking the bidding too high. If you are third or fourth in hand, the quality of the spade suit suggests an opening of one spade. If partner replies one no-trump you can now show the clubs, thereby guaranteeing you started with at least a five-card spade suit. But if you get a response of two diamonds or two hearts do not now bid three clubs! Facing a partner who has passed at his first turn to bid, you are heading for serious trouble by promising 16+ points.

5-4 Hands

The bidding of hands when you have adjacent suits of five- and four-card length, and the five-card suit is higher-ranking than the four-card one, presents no problems. You simply open with the longer suit and rebid the shorter:

(a) ♠ 7 3
    ♡ A Q 9 8 7
    ♢ K Q J 9
    ♣ J 4

(b) ♠ A 2
    ♡ A Q 9 8 7
    ♢ K Q J 9
    ♣ J 4

On hand (a) you open one heart, and whether partner responds one spade or two clubs, you rebid two diamonds. On hand (b) you have four points more, and you open one heart as on (a), but you have a choice of rebids. The old fashioned approach would be to bid three diamonds, forcing, and showing a strong hand. That takes up a lot of bidding space, and a simple two diamonds will hardly ever result in a missed game. A reasonable alternative that gets across the extra strength of your hand is two no trumps.

Hands with a five and a four-card suit, which are not adjacent, require a bit of care. Above all, don't just pick up your hand and bid without thinking what the future may have in store.

(c) ♠ K Q 9 8 2   (d) ♠ A Q 9 8 2   (e) ♠ K Q 9 8 2
    ♡ J 10 7   ♡ K 7 3   ♡ 8
    ◇ 8   ◇ 8   ◇ A K 7 5
    ♣ A K 7 5   ♣ A K 7 5   ♣ J 6 2

Hand (c) is not very strong. Obviously you open one spade and if partner responds two diamonds you can't make the one-round force of a rebid of three clubs, because partner will credit you with 16+ points, and whatever would you do if he then bid three diamonds? So you just rebid two spades and forget about wanting to show your club suit – if nothing else, your partner will know you have at least a five-card spade suit. Please note that you didn't rebid two spades 'to show a five-carder' – horrible phrase! – but because you couldn't rebid anything else. If instead of two diamonds, partner responds two hearts you, with the knowledge that he has a five-card heart suit, can raise to three hearts, a bid which promises no greater strength than a two spade rebid but which is more constructive.

Now compare hand (d) with hand (c). They have exactly the same shape so you open one spade. However, hand (d) has 16 points, so if partner responds two diamonds you are more than strong enough to show your second suit with a rebid of three clubs. But what if partner bids two hearts in response to your one spade? Be careful not to rebid three hearts, as you did on hand (c). It's not even forcing and a partner who has just managed to scrape up his two heart bid on 8 points and a five-card heart suit, might well pass. Say three clubs, showing a strong hand, and see what partner does next – he's bound to do something, as he must honour your forcing bid. A game contract is certain to be reached, almost surely in hearts. If your partner also has a good hand there may be a slam. If, over his two hearts bid, you go straight to four hearts instead of showing a minor suit at the three-level, you will have said that you hold just a spade-heart hand with too many minor suit losers for you to be interested in a slam. That isn't true of hand (d), is it? You have only one diamond loser and the two top clubs.

Hand (e) is a little bit tricky. You open one spade, of course, and can only rebid two spades if partner responds two hearts. However, if partner instead responds two clubs, don't make the mistake of bidding three clubs – show your second suit by bidding two diamonds. The difference between this hand and (c) is that partner's bid of two Hearts over your one spade guaranteed five hearts. His bid of two clubs, on the other hand, may have been made on a four-card suit, or just possibly only a three-card suit. So don't raise with only three-card support yourself.

4-5 Hands

We come now to a somewhat awkward matter, and that is how to cope with moderate hands where your four and five-card suits are adjacent, with the four-card suit the higher-ranking.

(a) ♠ K Q J 4	(b) ♠ Q	(c) ♠ K 2
♡ K 8 7 6 4	♡ A Q 9 2	♡ A 4
◇ 7	◇ K 9 7 4 2	◇ K J 9 2
♣ A J 9	♣ J 9 2	♣ Q 9 5 3 2

With hand (a) it is the quality of the spades that is disturbing, and formerly it would have been in order to open with a bid of one spade, and rebid two hearts, risking ending up in a 4-3 fit if partner gave you preference to spades. Nowadays an opening bid of one spade followed by a rebid in any other suit after partner has made a change of suit response, guarantees a five-card suit to which partner may return holding a doubleton – and trump fits of 4-2 are seldom comfortable! With weaker spades you would have no hankering to bid them and would just open one heart and over a minor suit response simply rebid two hearts. On the shape of hand shown in (a) rebid a quiet two hearts. If partner does have a four-card spade suit he would either have bid it before his minor suit, or be planning to make a responder's reverse into spades himself – and you'll have no problems knowing what to do then.

With hand (b) you have the same dilemma. To open with one heart and follow with two diamonds over a response of Two Clubs would guarantee a five-card heart suit, so, unless you are prepared to pass, One Diamond it has to be. If partner bids one spade over the one diamond, just rebid two diamonds. With only 12 points you are not nearly strong enough to rebid one no-trump. Make your jack of clubs the king and one no-trump would be a practical alternative.

Hand (c) might be opened with a bid of one no-trump. You may well pinch the contract. However, 5-4-2-2 is not a balanced distribution, so you do so at your peril. If your partner turns out to be 5-5 in the majors and expects to find you with at least three-card support for one of them, you will have some explaining to do! There is nothing wrong with opening one club and rebidding two clubs unless, of course, partner bids diamonds. If the opponents intervene you can pass showing the minimum nature of your hand.

4-4-4-1 Hands

Hands with three four-card suits and a singleton and less than 15 points are tricky to bid. A long-established method is to bid the suit ranked below the singleton unless the singleton is in clubs when you should always bid one heart. We say always, but be prepared to pay attention to suit quality, and given a choice between opening at the one level with say, ♡ 5-4-3-2 or ♣ A-K-Q-J, we know which suit we would choose! Another method is to bid the middle of the three four-card suits when they are touching and always bid one club when they are not. The difficulties arise when partner responds in the suit of the singleton. Holding sufficient points you can consider rebidding in no-trumps but if this would overstate the strength of the hand then bid the next suit up. Here are some examples for you:

(a) ♠ A Q 4 3   (b) ♠ 10   (c) ♠ A Q 4 3   (d) ♠ K J 9 2
    ♡ 9   ♡ A K 9 8   ♡ 9 7 6 2   ♡ Q J 6 3
    ◇ A J 8 2   ◇ J 10 8 4   ◇ A   ◇ K Q 7 4
    ♣ Q 8 6 2   ♣ A J 10 9   ♣ K 6 3 2   ♣ 10

On hand (a) the opening bid is either one diamond or one club according to the method you and partner choose and if the response is one heart the rebid is one spade. Hand (b) requires a bid of one heart or one diamond and a rebid of two clubs over the inevitable reply of one spade. Hand (c) is opened with one club with a heart rebid over one diamond and hand (d) with one heart and a two diamond rebid. The problems arise because by opening with a bid of one suit, and then offering a second suit as trumps, you are implying that the first-named suit is at least five cards in length. There is less of a problem with a rebid on any of the above hands when partner changes the suit to one which you can happily give a minimum raise and await developments. Increase your points to at least fifteen in all four examples and the rebid problem will go away! This is because you now have additional options in some situations. In our second example, you could rebid one no-trump if partner responds one spade. Raise a change of suit to one in which you have four-card support, possibly with a jump.

3

One-Level Opening Bids and Rebids with Balanced Hands

If you play a 12–14 point one no-trump opening bid you will never have a problem when your hand contains the right number of points and shape. As a beginner you should have been taught not to worry about opening with one little losing doubleton or trebleton in the hand. Now you must steel yourself to open one no-trump no matter where the points in the hand actually are. In modern Acol, if you open one of a suit and rebid in another after partner has changed the suit, you are stating that you do not have a balanced hand, i.e. 4-4-3-2, 4-3-3-3 or 5-3-3-2 (which would generally be opened or rebid in no-trumps). So naturally partner understands sequences such as 1♠ – 2♣ – 2◇ to be expressing a preference for finding a trump fit, shying away from no-trumps and therefore offering at least a 5-4 shape, if not 5-5 or even 6-5.

Here are some rules for you to follow. With two four-card major suits, always bid one heart. With two four-card divided suits, bid the major, i.e. with four spades and four diamonds, bid one spade, and with four hearts and four clubs, bid one heart. With two four-card black suits we suggest you open one spade. If the next player wants to bid a suit, he now has to do it at the two level. With two four-card minor suits, you can bid either. Some players always start with the weaker suit, hoping that the opponents will not lead it!

As your judgement develops, you may vary these rules to fit individual hands, but for the time being stick to them as good general principles.

Here are some opening hands:

(a) ♠ A Q 9 2	(b) ♠ K Q 5	(c) ♠ K J 5 3
♡ K J 10 6	♡ A 2	♡ Q 3
◇ K 9 2	◇ K 7 6 4	◇ A 9 8
♣ K 4	♣ A Q 6 4	♣ A Q 8 6

Hand (a) presents no problems. By opening one heart you won't miss a 4-4 heart fit or a spade fit, as partner can show a spade suit at once. If partner bids either minor at the two level you rebid two no-trumps, showing your 15–16 points with confidence, knowing that major suit contracts have been considered. If partner bids one no-trump in response to one heart, a pass is the odds-on bid. A raise to two no-trumps is very pushy when partner has only promised around 5–8 points.

Hand (b) is equally easy. You could open either of your minors, but if you end up in no-trumps you would prefer the opposition to attack in clubs rather than diamonds. We suggest you open one diamond. Reverse your minor-suit holdings and one club would be our choice. Over a response of one heart, one spade or two diamonds, rebid two no-trumps to show 17–18 points, and over two clubs you can jump to three no-trumps to show your values.

Hand (c) may appear tricky. To open one spade and rebid two no-trumps over a response of two hearts will describe your hand well, but will you be happy to say two no-trumps if partner responds to one spade with two diamonds or two clubs? You should be! You have a balanced hand, and you heart holding may prove to be both valuable and well placed if the opponents lead that suit.

Here are three more opening hands:

(d) ♠ K J 5 3	(e) ♠ 10 8	(f) ♠ A J
♡ 7 5 2	♡ A J 10 9	♡ A 9 7 4
◇ A Q 8 6	◇ A K 9 6	◇ A K 7 3
♣ A K	♣ A 6 2	♣ K 10 4

Hand (d) should be opened with a bid of one spade. If partner replies two hearts, do not raise in hearts. A bid of three hearts would be too weak for your point count (and imply a five-card spade suit), while to bid four hearts would rule out a contract of three no-trumps! There is no ruffing power in your hand, and no weak suit, so three no-trumps is probably a superior contract. If partner now corrects to four hearts he is showing a six-card suit and you will be happy to let him play there.

Hand (e) frightens the faint-hearted! You open one heart (correctly) and instead of the hoped-for one spade, you hear partner bid two of either minor. Just bid a calm two no-trumps and don't panic about your weak spades. Remember that partner promises at least 8 points and it's reasonable odds that he has a spade honour. Or maybe he has three small spades, and the opposition have four each and you have the other nine tricks.

Hand (f) is pretty straightforward. Open one heart and rebid three no-trumps over any simple change of suit response or a raise to two hearts. If partner jumps to three hearts, a small slam try with a bid of three spades is indicated. Six hearts might just be on.

Remember:

1   All balanced hands with 4-4-3-2 (or, of course, 4-3-3-3 or 5-3-3-2) shape should be either opened or rebid in no-trumps. You might make an exception for a hand with a very good five-card minor suit. With a five-card major, we suggest you steer clear of opening one no-trump, as it may prove to be difficult to locate a fit in that suit.

2   An opening bid of one of a suit, followed by a rebid in a new suit at the two level after partner has made a change-of-suit response, shows a hand of at least 5-4 or 5-5 shape.

3   An opening bid of one of a suit, followed by a rebid of one no-trump shows a balanced 15–16 points. A rebid of two no-trumps when partner's response has been at the two level shows the same 15–16 points.

4   If opener's balanced hand has 17–18 points, responder's bid at the one level must be followed by a rebid of two no-trumps. If responder has bid at the two level, opener must make a jump rebid of three no-trumps to show the same 17–18 points.

5   If opener's balanced hand contains 19 points, a jump to three no-trumps after a one level bid from responder will show them. If responder changes the suit at the two level, then opener may have to manufacture a forcing rebid in case there are slam possibilities on the hand.

1♡ 1♠		1♡ 2♣	
one no-trump = 15–16 points		2NT = 15–16 points	

1♡ 1♠		1♡ 2♣	
2NT = 17–18 points		3NT = 17–18 points	

4
Opener's Rebids

Opener's second call in the auction, his rebid, is the keystone of most auctions, particularly when the opening bid has been one of a suit. Whether or not you ultimately end in the right contract is going to depend on a number of factors. Did you choose the right opening bid? Can you depend on partner to have made the right response? Will you make the right decision as to your rebid? Have your opponents intervened in the auction, and have you placed the right interpretation on their bids or silence?

Before we go on to how you value your hand for your rebid, let's just take a few very elementary examples of how your opponents actions should influence your thinking. Perhaps the most elementary example one can think of would be a hand like (a) below:

(a) ♠ 7 6 4   (b) ♠ K J 5   (c) ♠ A K Q 10 9 5
    ♡ A Q 9 7 5   ♡ A Q 8 7 5   ♡ K Q 2
    ◇ K J 4   ◇ K 8   ◇ K 8 6
    ♣ K 7   ♣ 7 6 4   ♣ 8

You are on the left of the dealer and, when you pick up your hand and sort it, you have immediate visions of opening one heart when, much to your disgust, the dealer opens one no-trump (strong) before you've had a chance to speak. What do you do? You still have a perfectly good opening one heart hand, but now you have 15–17 points on your right. What do you do? Change step smartly and say no bid. Even if the no-trump had been weak (12–14 points), you would be wise to do the same. You have a broken suit, and no source of tricks if partner has a worthless hand. Move the king of clubs into the heart suit, and the situation changes. That would give you a perfectly reasonable overcall, whatever the range of the no-trump opening.

Now let's turn to hand (b). You see immediately that you have an opening bid of one heart (14 points counting one for 'shape' by way of the fifth heart). Being the dealer you bid it firmly, but your left-hand opponent comes in with a jump bid of two spades (strong). Even an intermediate intervening bid of one spade would make you change your mind about your strength for when the auction comes round to you again you will devalue your hand because you can no longer consider the ♠ K-J-5 as worth 4 points. If the auction goes in such a way that you are released from the necessity to rebid, you will grasp the opportunity to pass. If you must rebid, you will do so as conservatively as you can. Had your right-hand opponent been the dealer, and opened one spade before you, you would consider that your spades had gone up in value – the ♠ A-Q are most likely to be on your right, but you would still be running a risk by entering the auction with a bid of two hearts. Our view is that you need a better suit than this to overcall!

Lastly, take hand (c). Here, left to yourself, you would be intending to open one spade and, over any response from partner, jump to three spades. However, over your opening one spade, your left-hand opponent bids two diamonds, and two passes bring the auction back to you. Would you still bid three spades? Partner may have a few scattered values, but the spades may be stacked on your right, and in all probability your king of diamonds and one of your heart honours will be dead ducks. The best you can possibly do is repeat your spades at the two-level. That will at least tell partner you have a fair hand.

Rebidding on Moderate Hands in an Uncontested Auction

It is, very much easier for a partnership to communicate its values when the opponents do not enter the auction. So when this happens, make the most of it and select carefully the most descriptive and truthful bids. After a sequence such as 1♡ – 1♠, very little has so far been said except that one member of the partnership has an opening bid and the other a response. That may have been made on as little as 5 points whilst the opening bid may contain anything between 12 and 19. So far the right contract is anybody's guess. It is how opener views his cards in the light of the little he has gleaned from his partner which, more often than not, sets the seal on whether the hand will ultimately be played in a part-score, game, or even a slam.

When reviewing your hand, keep in mind a simple point. Is it within the range of 12–15, or 16–19?

Here we insist – and it can't be repeated too often – that you must never allow yourself to become 'point-bound'. The point count should only be used as a guideline. For example, if you found yourself looking at:

♠ K Q J 10 9 6
♡ A 8 4 2
◇ 7 3
♣ 5

you would certainly be correct to open one spade even though you only have 10 points.

You will find yourself picking up a good hand that must be downgraded, perhaps because the high cards are in your short suits, or particularly if an opposition bid has caused you to revise your trick taking potential.

You may have to go in the other direction, upgrading a hand, possibly because of an opposition bid or because you have a lot of high intermediates, eights, nines and tens.

If you open with one of a suit and your partner responds with a simple one-over-one or two-over-one bid, and you decide that your hand fits on the left-hand side of the imaginary line, you have the choice of only four bids:

1   Rebid your own suit at the lowest available level, 1◇ – 1♡ – 2◇. This will be on a single-suited hand, and partner will now know that you have the weakest possible hand, one-suited, but that your suit is at least five cards in length.

2   Support your partner's suit with a single raise, 1◇ – 1♡ – 2♡ or 1♠ – 2♡ – 3♡. You promise him a four-card fit, of course, but with one exception – do you remember it? Yes, it is if you opened one spade and partner responded two hearts. Now if you raise to three hearts you show a moderate hand with at least three hearts. (We recently encountered a player with more than 30 years' experience who did not know that a response of two hearts to one spade guarantees at least a five-card suit!)

3   Show a second suit, lower ranking than your first bid suit, 1◇ – 1♡ – 2♣. This bid doesn't promise any extra strength, but it does offer partner a choice of trump suit and asks him to say which he prefers.

4   Rebid in no-trumps at the lowest available level, $1\heartsuit - 1\spadesuit - 1NT$ or $1\heartsuit$ $- 2\clubsuit - 2NT$. Here we have a rebid that goes right across the middle of our mental line. Before you can get this absolutely into your heads you will have to read Chapter 5, 'More About Opener's Rebids', because if you are using a strong no-trump, a rebid of one no-trump, as in our first example sequence, shows 12–14 points. So what we are really talking about is when you are using a weak no-trump opening which means that a no-trump rebid as in either of our example sequences, shows 15–16 points. It will hardly ever arise if you are using a strong no-trump because you will have opened one no-trump in the first place. In that case the no-trump rebid being at the lowest level, shows the same type of hand, balanced, with 12–14 points.

So, you see, it's really quite simple. If you don't hold more than a moderate hand with 15 points at best, you must choose your rebid from one of the four choices set out above, the only possible exception being No 4, which can go up to 16 points if you make your rebid in no-trumps.

5

More About Opener's Rebids

Make sure you understand Chapter 4 before you study this chapter, which deals with the group of hands which fall on the right-hand side of the mental line, the 16–19 point hands. You will occasionally have a hand with an even higher point count that can only be opened with a one-bid, but they do not appear very often, so we draw the line at 19 points.

The stronger your hand, the more options you will have as to how to bid it. Remember that this group of hands, though stronger than the ones we have already dealt with, is limited by the fact that, either because of the point count or 'shape', you couldn't make a stronger opening bid than at the one-level. Your partner, therefore, already knows that you were unable to open with two clubs or a strong two bid.

Never deceive your partner. If his total points and your announced limit (if you have made a rebid showing a moderate hand) don't arrive somewhere close to the required values for the game you are considering bidding, he won't make another bid if he feels the right place for a part-score has been found. However, he won't be pleased when you and he end up with ten tricks and you have only contracted to make Two Hearts!

Now for some bids you can make with a 16 points plus hand:

1 Rebid your own suit with a single jump in level, 1♠ – 2♢ – 3♠. This jump rebid tells partner you have a good six-card suit in a single-suited hand, and that you expect to make seven tricks with it if the hand is played in your suit. Note that we haven't actually mentioned points, but you will find it difficult to construct a hand to fit the bid that doesn't contain 16+ points if you include your distributional values.

2 Raise partner's suit with a jump in level, 1♡ – 1♠ – 3♠. But be careful! If you hold hand (a) below, then you would open one club and raise partner's response of one spade to three spades. But that doesn't force

him to bid one more for game, and if he just managed to scrape up enough to say his one spade, you would be in the right part-score. But if the hand on which you opened your one club looks like (b), then you must raise that one spade response straight to game.

(a) ♠ K J 8 7   (b) ♠ K J 8 7
    ♡ K 2   ♡ K 2
    ◇ A 7 2   ◇ A 7 2
    ♣ A 10 9 8   ♣ A K 10 9

In passing it is worth pointing out that these two rebids, whilst being limit bids, are not 'shut-out' bids. If partner is strong for his first response, it is up to him to note what you have told him, and make another forward move, possibly towards a slam.

3   If you have a balanced hand and no fit for your partner's suit, make your rebid in no-trumps, 1♣ – 1♡ – 2NT or 1♠ – 2◇ – 3NT. With 17–18 points, after a one-level response, jump to two no-trumps. Had partner bid at the two-level he would, of course, have told you he had a good 8–9 points, so you would have bid the game immediately. Had you been lucky enough to have picked up 19 points yourself, then all you would be waiting for is any sort of squeak from partner to be in game, so you may go straight to three no-trumps even over a one-level response. Again, don't think that you are making a 'shut-out' bid – far from it! You are telling partner that you have a balanced hand totalling 19 points, and if he feels there is possibly more than a game on he may make any sort of slam try he likes.

4   You may 'reverse', that is, bid a lower-ranking suit before a higher-ranking one, 1♡ – 2◇ – 2♠, but only on a special type of hand. Don't do this before you have read and learned the requirements, both from opener's and responder's points of view, which are set out on pages 28 and 36.

5   As you will see when we go into 'reverses', you often have a two-suited hand, and when your first suit doesn't appeal to partner, you want to offer him the other. Show your new suit at the three-level, 1◇ – 1♡ – 3♣ or 1♠ – 2♣ – 3♡. A new suit bid at the three-level is unconditionally forcing for one round, and you should never be left there just because partner prefers your second suit to your first. He must make another bid.

We shall have more to say about these three-level rebids towards the end of this section. Meanwhile, let's return to No 4, the 'reverse'.

Reverse Rebids

The definition of an opener's reverse is, quite simply, a bid in a new suit that forces responder to go to the three-level to show simple preference. The requirements are a strong hand of around 16 or more points, and two suits, the lower ranking of which is longer than the higher-ranking. The bid is unconditionally forcing for one round and responder should generally rebid in no-trumps according to his strength if he has the fourth suit well stopped. Failing that, he should give a raise of opener's second suit, simple preference for his first, or jump preference showing real support and better than minimum for his bidding thus far.

A few examples should help to make this clear:

(a) ♠ A K J 7   (b) ♠ A J 9 5   (c) ♠ 3
    ♡ K Q J 8 4   ♡ A Q 9 7 2   ♡ A Q 9 5
    ◇ 9   ◇ K 8 3   ◇ A K J 8 7
    ♣ K 10 5   ♣ 6   ♣ K 10 4

On hand (a) open one heart and, over a two club or two diamond response, reverse into two spades, showing a minimum of 16 points with the first-bid suit longer than the second. This makes life very easy for responder, who, with the knowledge that your hearts are longer than your spades, can choose the right major, go back to his minor, or rebid in no-trumps if he holds the unbid suit well stopped. Note, that the responder can also use 'fourth suit forcing' (see Chapter 10) if he wants to ask opener to describe his hand further.

With hand (b) you are not strong enough to reverse. If you do, your partner will forever think you have a minimum of 16 points, and it will be your fault if the bidding goes too high. Deal with it as set out in Chapter 2, the section on 4-5 hands.

On hand (c) your choice is equally easy. Simply open one diamond and reverse into two hearts over your partner's expected one spade, or possible two club response. If he were to bid one heart, a jump to four hearts would not be an overstatement of your values.

New Suit Bid at the Three-Level

You will find the new suit bid at the three-level, which is unconditionally forcing, is most useful. You may introduce a minor suit bid, without a four-card holding, if your hand simply can't be expressed in any other way. Let's look at some examples and choose the best rebid on each:

(a) ♠ A K Q 8 5 4   (b) ♠ A K J 9 4   (c) ♠ K 7 4
    ♡ A 7   ♡ A Q J 9 3   ♡ A K 10 5 2
    ◇ K J 4   ◇ Q 5   ◇ 3 2
    ♣ 4 3   ♣ 7   ♣ A Q J

On hand (a) you open one spade and rebid three spades over whatever partner says. Playing weak two bids, this must be unconditionally forcing. Partner knows you have a six-card suit, and can raise you to four spades with a couple of little spades and something outside. Notice, how important it is not to rebid your own suit at the three-level, unless you have a six-card suit.

Hand (b) is easy too. You open one spade, and unless you get a response of two hearts, rebid three hearts over whatever partner says. All you want to know is which is his better major, as you hope to play in game in it. Remember he can't pass, so he will either give you preference to three spades or raise to four hearts or four spades. Occasionally, if hating your suits, he will rebid his own or go into no-trumps.

Hand (c), needs a closer look. If partner replies one spade to your opening one heart, you have an awkward rebid to find. Two hearts is too weak for this 17-point hand. Three hearts would promise six hearts. You have no second suit to offer. What about no-trumps? Rather dangerous with that little doubleton diamond! Still, it reflects the playing strength and balanced nature of the hand, and two no-trumps gets our vote.

Now look at these three hands, any of which is right for your partner's original bid of one spade:

(a) ♠ A Q J 5   (b) ♠ A Q J 5   (c) ♠ A Q J 5
    ♡ 8 4 3   ♡ J 4 3   ♡ 4 3
    ◇ J 9 4   ◇ J 9 4   ◇ A Q 4 2
    ♣ 9 6 2   ♣ K 6 2   ♣ 8 7 2

Hands (a) and (b) are exactly the same shape – and three no-trumps is certainly a playable contract. Even if the opponents lead a diamond, you may survive if the suit divides 4-4. On hand (c) your partner has enough in diamonds to make you reasonably confident that you will make your game.

Finally, here are three more hands that responder might hold for his one spade bid. What should he do when the bidding goes 1♡ – 1♠ – 2NT?

(d) ♠ A Q J 10 6   (e) ♠ A Q J 10 6 2   (f) ♠ A Q 8 2
    ♡ 6 4   ♡ 3   ♡ 3 2
    ◇ 6 4   ◇ K 7 5   ◇ 9 8 5
    ♣ K 9 4 3   ♣ 9 7 3   ♣ K 8 3 2

On (d) partner will bid a forcing three spades, in the hope that you will like your hand well enough to raise to game. On (e) he is quite good enough to jump-rebid his spades to game.

Hand (f) is a raise to three no-trumps.

6
Responder Bids and Rebids

Your beginners' book will have gone in some detail into the first principles of responding so we just list here a few reminders.

1 If partner opens one heart or one spade and you have four-card support, make a limit raise, a delayed game raise, or, with 16 plus points (combining honour points and distribution) make a jump bid in a new suit (1 ♡ – 3 ♣) which is unconditionally forcing to game.

2 If you have a suit of your own you want to show, you may do so at the one-level with as little as 5 or 6 points, but if you are forced to bid at the two-level (1 ♠ – 2 ♢) you must hold a minimum of nine points.

3 Remember that in Acol you don't make a change-of-suit response to a bid of one heart or one spade if your hand falls within the confines of a limit bid (up to 12 points) as to do so would deny the holding of four of partner's major.

4 With a balanced hand make a limit response in no-trumps according to the number of points you hold, provided you lack four-card support for partner's major suit, and if bidding two no-trumps or three no-trumps, you have an honour in each of the unbid suits.

This is a good moment to remind you that Acol players don't give limit raises to partner's minor suit openings as often as they do to major suits. This is not to say that you must never make a limit raise of partner's minor suit opening, but only do so if you have nothing possibly more constructive to say. The point is that you don't want to climb all the way up the attic stairs to an eleven-trick contract in clubs or diamonds when nine tricks in no-trumps are there for the taking, and a change-of-suit response may get you there when a limit bid wouldn't.

A few examples should brush away any cobwebs.

(a) ♠ A Q 9 6   (b) ♠ 9 7 6   (c) ♠ K 7 6
    ♡ 8 4   ♡ Q 8 2   ♡ Q 8 2
    ◇ 4 3 2   ◇ Q 7 4   ◇ Q 7 4
    ♣ Q 7 6 4   ♣ Q 7 6 4   ♣ Q 7 6 4

On hand (a) the obvious response to partner's one club is one spade –
don't fall into the trap of bidding two clubs. The latter would be
completely non-constructive, whilst one spade might be just what
partner wanted to hear to go into no-trumps. But remember that an Acol
player who bids one club often has spades as his second suit. If he
doesn't care for your spades and elects to rebid in a red suit you can
always 'correct' to clubs.

'Correcting', which is merely putting partner back to his first bid suit,
does not constitute a raise. On hand (b), you have just enough to squeak
two clubs in response to partner's one club, with the hope that this will
be pre-emptive enough to make it difficult for your left-hand opponent
to come in at the two-level. At any rate you will have warned partner
that you have the weakest possible hand for him, guaranteeing four
clubs and a minimum of 5 points.

You will note that on hand (b) we have told you to respond to one club
with two clubs and not with one no-trump. That is the right response to
one club on hand (c), twelve cards of which are exactly the same as hand
(b). The thirteenth is the nine of spades that has become the king, which
is all-important. A response of one no-trump to one club shows a
balanced hand of 8–10 points, which may or may not contain four-card
club support or a four-card diamond suit. It will not, however, contain a
four-card major, because you always take the opportunity to show
partner four hearts or spades if you can – you don't want to miss a
possible 4–4 major suit fit or no-trump contract.

Following the same principle, the sequence 1◇ – 1NT shows around
5–8/9 points and you would use 1◇ – 2◇ only on the weakest end of
the range with a hand containing four-card diamond support. If you
return to the example hands on the previous page, and mentally
exchange the diamond and club suits, you will see what we mean. On
(b) you would raise one Diamond to two Diamonds as you have
absolutely nothing in spades. On (c) one no-trump would be by far the
best response. Both bids again deny a four-card major suit.

Responder Has Two Four-Card Suits

There are, of course, many occasions on which there is no question of making a limit bid in response to partner's opening, either in his suit or in no-trumps. You intend, in fact, to make a change-of-suit response that, unless you have previously passed, is a one-round force. If you have just one suit to bid, you have no problems, though you must bear in mind, that if your suit has to be bid at the two-level (1♠ – 2◇) you must have a good 9 points. It is when you have two suits of equal length that the matter of choice arises. If these suits are both of four-card length, you show them in ascending order, that is, you bid the lower-ranking first provided you lack a four-card major, which you must never conceal.

(a) ♠ Q 9 8 5   (b) ♠ K Q 8 5   (c) ♠ J 3
    ♡ J 10 7 6   ♡ K J 8 4   ♡ 7 4 2
    ◇ K 7 2   ◇ K 7 2   ◇ K J 7 2
    ♣ 8 4   ♣ 8 4   ♣ A 10 8 4

On hand (a) you have just enough to muster up a response to partner's opening bid of one of a minor, and on hand (b) you have ample – enough, in fact, to intend to make a forward-going bid on the next round, whatever partner's rebid. However, on both you will respond one heart and wait to hear partner's rebid. The reason for bidding one heart and not one spade is because you want to give yourself and partner the best possible chance to find a fit, if you have one. On hand (a) you are so weak that game is extremely unlikely, and you don't want to allow the auction to get too high before finding the right spot to play for a part-score. With hand (b), however, you have every expectation of playing in a game contract, either a major suit or no-trumps. By bidding one heart on both hands you will find out if opener, has four hearts, because if he has, he will at once make a limit bid in support of your suit. If he has spades you have left him room to show them at the one-level over your one heart bid, however weak his opening hand was. However, if you choose to bid one spade on either hand, you will very possibly get yourself and partner into all sorts of trouble – and partner won't be pleased with you!

Hand (a) is worth only one bid from you, and unless partner makes a forcing rebid, you won't speak again, except to give preference if the bidding has gone 1◇ – 1♡ – 2♣. Don't get careless with hand (b) just because you can certainly find another bid whatever partner rebids. If you bid one spade in answer to his opening one diamond, and he now rebids two diamonds, and you now bid two hearts, you guarantee that you hold at least five spades and four hearts, precisely because you bid the spades before the hearts.

So with hand (b) just bid one heart and wait to hear what partner rebids. If he replies with two hearts or three hearts, your hand is now worth 13 points, and you will bid game in hearts. If he rebids one spade, again your hand is worth 13 points, and you will bid the game in spades. If his opening bid were one club, and over your one heart he rebids two clubs, you will know he doesn't hold four spades, or he would have told you so. When you have an opening bid of your own facing an opening bid from partner, you should generally try for game. However, there is nothing stopping partner from having a minimum, and with no useful club honour, you should bid two no-trumps. Partner will go to game unless he has the minimum hand you are worried about. Similarly, if he had opened one diamond, and rebid two clubs over your one heart, don't make the error of busily bidding against him in the major suits whilst he bids in the minors. Bid two no-trumps, and leave the rest to your partner.

Now let's consider the situation when the opening bid has been one diamond, and over your response of one heart partner just rebids two diamonds. Now you know you have no major suit fit, but you also know that between you there are probably enough points for game. The question is where? Don't blindly bid two no-trumps, because partner will trust you for something in clubs and may well raise to three no-trumps with, say, ♣ Q-x-x, and the defence may well wrap up the first five tricks in clubs! Raise to three diamonds and if partner cannot make another bid, it is unlikely that game will have been missed.

Look back to example hand (c). Your correct response to an opening bid of one heart or one spade is two clubs, the lower ranking of your two four-card suits. Now if opener has a second suit of diamonds, he will show it, and a fit has been found. But if you carelessly bid two diamonds over a major suit opening, and opener's second suit is clubs, he will have to go to the three-level to show it. A new suit bid at the three-level is forcing, showing a strong hand, so if partner hasn't got a strong hand he won't be able to bid three clubs and the club fit may be missed.

Responder Has Two Five-Card Suits

All we have said in these last pages has concerned what you should do with
two four-card suits, but what about two five-card suits, particularly the
majors, when partner opens with one of a minor? Well, you naturally want
to offer him the choice of either, so once again you must bid in the most
economical way, especially if your hand is not very strong in points.

(a) ♠ A J 10 8 6   (b) ♠ 7   (c) ♠ 7
    ♡ K 9 7 6 4   ♡ J 2   ♡ A K J 8 6
    ◇ 7   ◇ A J 10 8 6   ◇ J 2
    ♣ J 2   ♣ K 9 7 6 4   ♣ K Q 7 6 4

Look at hand (a). You have only 9 high-card points, but if you can find
partner with three cards of either major, after he has opened one club or
one diamond, you will make a comfortable part-score, or game if he is
strong, once you have found your fit. Bid one spade to start with (note that
this is the exact opposite of responding with two four-card suits). Now if
he rebids in a minor, you will be able to bid two hearts. But if you start with
a response of one heart over one club or one diamond, and hear a rebid of
either minor, now if you rebid two spades you will have incorrectly made
a responder's reverse. Partner will never understand that you started with
five hearts and five spades, and will expect a much stronger hand. By
bidding the spades first and then showing the hearts you guarantee at least
five spades and four hearts, precisely because if both were four-card suits
you would have showed the hearts first.

Now look at hand (b). Here your five-card suits are in the minors and your
point count is exactly the same 9. If partner opens one heart or one spade,
and you follow the same principle as with hand (a) and bid the higher-
ranking suit first, you may well miss a club fit. The point is that if partner,
for example, rebids two spades, you are not strong enough to bid three
clubs, which would be a one-round force – and think how you would feel
if partner's next rebid were three spades! So bid two clubs as your first
reply and if partner makes a weak rebid of his major suit, just say 'no bid'
(sometimes the most difficult bid in bridge!). The hands don't fit, and your
partner will have trouble getting anywhere near eight tricks in spades, or
even hearts. But suppose on hand (b) your jack of hearts were to become
the ace. Now, of course, you will treat these two five-card minor suits as
you did the two five-card majors in hand (a), and so you bid two diamonds
first and then show the club suit at the three level. When responder

introduces a new suit at the three level, it is a one-round force, exactly as when opener does that, so you cannot get left in three clubs.

Hand (c) presents no problems over an opening of one diamond from partner. Show the heart suit first, and introduce the clubs at the appropriate level according to opener's rebid. Over an opening one spade from partner, show the hearts first (guaranteeing five, of course) and then bid the clubs. However, take away your ace of hearts and substitute the two and now you have only 10 points. If opener rebids two spades you must pass! The hand is a misfit and disaster lurks if you press on ever higher.

Responder's Reverse

In the previous chapter we established very clearly the requirements for a reverse bid made by opener – i.e. a hand of strength and quality, with 16 plus high-card points, or compensating distribution, and with at least one more card in the first-bid and lower-ranked suit than in the second. Now we come to a responder's reverse that requires 12–13 points and, again, one more card in the first-bid and lower-ranked suit than in the second. Some examples:

(a) ♠ A Q 8	(b) ♠ A Q 8 3	(c) ♠ A Q 8 3
♡ K Q 10 9 8	♡ 8 3	♡ 8 3
◇ 7 3 2	◇ A Q 7 4 3	◇ Q 7 5 4 2
♣ J 4	♣ 7 2	♣ 10 4

With hand (a) partner opens one club and over your one heart rebids two clubs. Your reverse bid into two spades confirms your five-card heart suit and a good hold on spades, though it does not guarantee a four-card holding. This is because you both know that opener does not have a four-card spade suit himself – for then he would have rebid one spade and not two clubs. Your bid is forcing for one round and you hope that opener can now show three-card support for your hearts, or bid no-trumps if he has something in diamonds. Now you hold hand (b) and partner's opening is one heart. You are strong enough to bid two diamonds and reverse into two spades over a probable rebid of two hearts. This time you are guaranteeing a four-card spade suit. If partner has opened on a weak hand with four spades and five hearts, he would not have been able to reverse into two spades himself, but can now raise you in spades, knowing there is an eight-card fit. Be careful with hand (c). If partner opens one club you can bid a natural one diamond and await his rebid. If that rebid is two clubs, pass! If you were now to show spades, you are making a responder's reverse for which you have the shape but nowhere near the points. If partner opens one diamond show your spades and see what happens next, planning to return to diamonds with your next bid. But if partner opens one heart, bid one spade not two diamonds or a possible spade fit could be lost. Or maybe he has a balanced hand lacking values in spades and he doesn't dare to rebid in no-trumps. If partner reverts to two hearts, pass. If you now bid your diamonds you will have drawn a picture of a hand with a five-card spade suit and at least 12 points. Disaster will ensue!

7
More About Responder's Role

If you read back over the sections on Opener's Rebids you will remember that we advised opener to think of his hand as falling into one of two categories, moderate, that is 12–15 points, and strong, that is 16–19 points. Borderline hands, of 15–16 points, we value up or down according to whether they have good 'intermediaries' and according to responder's first bid. Remember, with hands of 20 points or more we try to open with something better than a one bid, so for practical purposes, if you open with a one bid you are denying the ability to make a stronger opening, and responder will react accordingly.

Now we tell you, as responder, not to divide your hand into two categories as opener did, but into one of three categories. First come weak holdings, limited to 6–9 points, on which you will only make one bid unless opener forces you to bid again. Second come intermediate holdings, 10–12 points, on which you may well want to make more than one bid, and third, hands on which you would have opened the bidding yourself had you been first or second caller. Don't be too rigid about these point ranges – as always, they are only a guide, and a hand can turn out to be worth either more or less than your original view of it, depending on opener's rebid and any bids that may come in from the opposition.

It follows, doesn't it, that if you hold a weak hand and opener shows only a moderate hand when he rebids, you will only bid again to give preference if necessary? If you hold a moderate hand and so does opener, game may still be on, and you will probably want to make a second try if you have something sensible to suggest. Holding a hand itself worth an opening bid, you will either bid game straight away if you know where that game lies, or make some forcing response if you need more information. Unless there seems to be a total misfit – in which case pass as quickly as possible! – the old saying 'an opening bid opposite an opening bid means a game somewhere' holds true. Should you have an absolutely super hand, even though opener shows only a moderate hand on his rebid, you may still be interested in the possibilities of a slam. We'll discuss that in more detail in Chapter 13.

6–9 Point Responding Hands

Each of the following responding hands falls into our first category, weak and not worth more than one bid unless opener shows strength on his rebid:

(a) ♠ K 8 7 4	(b) ♠ 9	(c) ♠ 8 7
♡ 6 4	♡ A J 9 8 7 3	♡ K 7 4 2
◇ K 9 8 6 3	◇ 3 2	◇ Q J 2
♣ 5 4	♣ J 6 5 3	♣ Q 5 4 2

Hand (a) is a response of one diamond if partner opens one club. If he rebids two clubs, say 'no bid'. If the opening bid is one diamond or one heart, you can respond one spade – note that this is far superior to raising one diamond to two diamonds. You cannot, of course, even consider bidding two diamonds over one heart! If the opening bid had been one spade, you would be delighted to bid a simple two spades. No matter what rebid opener makes, only bid again, other than to give simple preference (which is not a raise) if the rebid is unconditionally forcing.

Hand (b) is a tricky one if partner's opening is one spade! There is only one response you can make and that is one no-trump. A bid from you of two hearts would promise far better values (and what would you do if partner's rebid was a jump to three diamonds!). If, over one no-trump, you hear two spades, pass. Opener has now guaranteed six spades and you must let him get on with the hand. If partner rebids two clubs, again pass happily, but if he rebids two diamonds you can now show your hearts without deceiving him as to your strength. On the rare occasion that the rebid is two hearts, we are sure you will have no problem jumping to four hearts!

Hand (c) is not difficult. If the opening bid is one spade it is an obvious one no-trump, and after one heart it is a raise to two hearts. But over either minor suit opening, bid one heart. Do not make the mistake of raising one club to two clubs, or of bidding one no-trump 'to show my 6–9 points,' in both cases wrongly denying possession of your four-card heart suit.

10–12 Point Responding Hands

The next group of examples comes into our second category of intermediate responding hands:

(a) ♠ Q 8 6   (b) ♠ 5 2   (c) ♠ 8 6
    ♡ 6 4 2   ♡ A K 8 5 2   ♡ K Q 9 8
    ◇ Q 2   ◇ K 6 4   ◇ J 4
    ♣ A K 6 5 2   ♣ J 4 2   ♣ A Q 8 7 6

As responder on hand (a), if partner opens one heart or one spade, your original reply must, of course, be two clubs. If he rebids his major (1♡ – 2♣ – 2♡) or bids the other, lower-ranking major (1♠ – 2♣ – 2♡), in the first sequence bid make an invitational raise to three hearts, and in the second give jump preference to three spades. If the bidding goes 1♠ – 2♣ – 3♡, bid Four Spades, a jump preference bid now that partner has guaranteed five spades. If instead it had been 1♡ – 2♣ – 2♠ (a reverse from opener) again give jump preference to the announced five-card major. If opener jump rebids the same major, then a raise to game is easy to find. But suppose partner rebids two no-trumps over our two clubs response. No matter which major he opened with, bid three of it. This promises three-card support only. Had you had four of his major originally you would either have raised directly to the three level or now be jumping into four hearts/four spades (delayed game raise). So if partner has a five-card major suit when he rebids two no-trumps to show his reasonably balanced 15–16 point hand, he can choose between game in the known eight-card major suit fit, or three no-trumps. Note that your bid is unconditionally forcing to game.

Had the opening bid been one club a jump to three clubs would be the best you could do. Over an opening bid of one diamond, if your response of two clubs attracts a simple rebid of two diamonds, you must chose between an aggressive two no-trumps, or a slightly conservative pass.

On hand (b), if partner opens one spade and rebids two spades, after your two heart response, try a rebid of two no-trumps to suggest a game. If you next hear three spades you are likely to be facing a six-card suit, and should raise to game. If the opening bid were one club or one diamond and after your response of one heart opener simply rebids his minor, again pass. You don't have enough high-card points to consider a minor suit game, you would be most ill advised to insist on playing in hearts by rebidding the suit, and no-trumps would be a real gamble, as partner's spade holding may be as flimsy as your own!

Hand (c) is another example of a responder's reverse. If partner opens one diamond or one spade, show your club suit, and if he simply rebids in his original suit, reverse into hearts. Do not make the mistake over an opening of one diamond of showing your hearts first and then your clubs on the next round. Partner will expect you to hold a five-card heart suit.

It is worth noting here that if opener changes the suit when he rebids, your reverse into the fourth suit does not guarantee that it is genuine. Chapter 10 explains the meanings attached to these 'fourth suit forcing' bids in detail.

13–15 Point Responding Hands

Now we come to the strong responding hands. The first thing we want to stress here is that there is no hurry to get to game. Unless you know precisely what denomination you want to bid it in, go slowly to find out what you need to know from partner – many a slam can be made on a very good two-suit fit with far fewer high-card points than you might think you need. To make a jump bid into a new suit responder must know where he intends to play and that it is merely a question of at how high a level.

So let's look at how best to treat some hands where we know there ought to be a game somewhere once partner has opened the bidding:

(a) ♠ Q 8 7 5   (b) ♠ 4 2   (c) ♠ A Q J 10 7 4 2 (d) ♠ A K 7 4
    ♡ 4   ♡ 7 2   ♡ 9 4   ♡ 8 5 3
    ◇ A K 7 4   ◇ A K 8 6 3   ◇ K 5   ◇ 7
    ♣ A J 10 2   ♣ A Q 7 4   ♣ J 4   ♣ K Q 8 4 2

With hand (a) if partner opens one heart just bid one spade, and over a rebid in hearts, or two of either minor, simply jump to three no-trumps. If the opening is one club or one diamond, show your spades and hope his rebid is one no-trump, which you can raise to three no-trumps. If partner raises you to two spades, then jump to four spades. If he raises you to three spades, then look for a slam, either by means of cue bidding or a Blackwood four no-trump bid. If the minor suit opening is rebid, then the simple approach is to simply bid the minor suit game. The heart weakness is too glaring to look for a no-trump contract. However, if partner starts with one spade don't raise his suit at all – yet. Change the suit to two clubs and await the rebid. Over any simple rebid, up to the level of two no-trumps, now jump to four spades, a delayed game raise. But beware if the rebid is a strong one. To jump now to four spades will be a limit sign-off. It is up to you to make a slam try and a Blackwood four no-trumps may well be the best way forward. Yes, we realise you haven't mentioned your spade support but partner will get a pleasant surprise when he finds he is to play the contract!

Hand (b) with all its strength in the minors is not attractive when partner opens one spade. However, you have opening values yourself and there ought to be a game somewhere. You try two diamonds and sure enough he rebids two spades. Say three clubs – a new suit at the three-level and unconditionally forcing – and hope partner can find a little something in hearts and say three no-trumps. If he retreats to three spades then raise to four spades. Of course, if partner had rebid two hearts instead of repeating his spades three clubs would become 'fourth suit forcing'. You should simply bid three no-trumps. If his rebid is two no-trumps, again try three clubs to pinpoint your five-card diamond suit, and respect a sign-off in three no-trumps. Just occasionally if he knows your shape of hand, partner may be able to look for a minor suit slam.

Hand (c) is not good enough for an immediate force of two spades over a one-level opening from partner. Bid one spade and then rebid four spades over his rebid no matter what it is. Now partner knows you have an excellent suit and he may be able to bid on.

Hand (d) is deceptive. If you respond two clubs to an opening bid of one diamond or one heart, the spade suit may get lost if the opener is not strong enough to introduce it. If you bid one spade, unless partner has a very strong hand, failing to mention the clubs will not necessarily be fatal. If you finish up in no-trumps, they are bound to be useful.

8
Pre-emptive Bidding

Your first bridge book will have told you quite a lot about making a pre-emptive opening bid, which is aimed solely at disrupting the bidding of your opponents, by robbing them of several rounds of bidding space, and we gave you examples of suitable hands. So, before we go on to learning more about the art of pre-empting, let's recap the most important points about pre-empts.

1   Pre-emptive bids are ideally made in third position after two passes, that is, when you know your partner hasn't the values for an opening bid. But don't be put off from making a pre-empt first or second in hand if you have the right cards.

2   There is no such thing as a weak pre-empt fourth in hand, as it would be pointless to try to block the bidding of three players who have already passed.

3   The hand will usually contain a seven or eight card suit, preferably with all its points, such as they are, in that suit. If the total point count goes above eight or nine, the hand is too strong for a pre-empt.

4   The hand will be virtually useless in defence, but played in the suit bid should produce about seven playing tricks if vulnerable and six if not vulnerable.

We are sure that all of you will know about weak three bids, but before we go on to discuss those, we want to introduce you to something new..

Weak Two Bids

The American Howard Schenken was undoubtedly one of the best players ever. He won three Bermuda Bowls.

One of his many contributions to the game was the development of the weak two-bid a convention that is now played the world over.

In the early days of bridge a great deal of attention was lavished on the use of opening bids at the two level to describe strong hands, exactly as in the Acol two bids that you will all be familiar with. Although 'strong two's' can be very effective when they come along, Schenken realised that they simply didn't occur often enough to devote several bids to them. By including the strong hands in an opening bid of two clubs the remaining suit bids at the two level are available to describe a different type of hand that appears with much greater frequency.

Schenken's original idea was to use the opening bids of two hearts and two spades to show a weak hand with a six-card suit. It was soon appreciated that two diamonds could also be used in the same way.

Being able to start the bidding more often inevitably presents your opponents with additional problems they would rather do without. It is no wonder that Schenken's suggestion has been almost universally adopted.

The weak two has become a fearsome weapon in the hands of modern players, who often pay little regard to suit quality and sometimes have only a five-card suit.

The range for a weak two can vary quite a lot depending on style and vulnerability but 5–10/11 points is a reasonable guide. With less than ten points it is likely your side has less than its fair share of the high cards. If your partner is a passed hand it becomes an absolute certainty. A preemptive bid risks incurring a penalty, but you hope it will save you points by comparison to whatever contract your opponents might make.

You are prepared to sacrifice some points in an attempt to stop your opponents bidding a game or perhaps even a slam. By starting the bidding at a high level, you make it difficult for your opponents to exchange information and they will sometimes have to resort to guesswork. Nobody guesses right all the time!

Every now and then you will catch your partner with a good hand and they will have the problem. At least they will have a good idea about the nature of your hand.

To make a preemptive bid you ideally need a reasonable number of tricks in your suit – that will give you some protection against a big penalty if you are doubled. However, since part of your strategy is to make life difficult for your opponents, you may sometimes take a calculated risk.

Now let's look at some examples.

(a) ♠ A Q J 8 5 3   (b) ♠ 9 2   (c) ♠ A 8 3
    ♡ 7 4   ♡ K Q 8 6 5 2   ♡ 7 5 2
    ◊ 10 7 3   ◊ 8 5 3   ◊ Q 10 9 8 6 4
    ♣ 8 4   ♣ K 6   ♣ 8

Example (a) would be a perfect two spade bid at any vulnerability. Your points are concentrated in your suit and you are likely to make five tricks all on your own. In (b), the suit is not so good this time so bidding carries more risk. In the interests of trying to make life difficult for your opponents you should take one and open two hearts. In (c), your suit is worse still in terms of high cards but the intermediates make two diamonds a reasonable choice.

(d) ♠ Q 8 7 6 4 2   (e) ♠ A Q J 8 5 3   (f) ♠ A Q J 8 5 3
    ♡ 7 4   ♡ Q 8 7 4   ♡ Q 8 7 4
    ◊ K 8 6 4   ◊ 5 3   ◊ 5 4 3
    ♣ 6   ♣ 4   ♣ —

In (d), your suit is dreadful but at favourable vulnerability we have seen many players try two spades. In (e) you have a good suit and the right values but holding four cards in the other major is a considerable flaw because your partner won't expect it. It usually works better to pass on this type of hand, hoping to bid later on. In (f), we have changed the four of clubs into a diamond. This time you have two 'flaws': the four-card heart suit and the club void. Two flaws are one too many and that rules out an opening bid of two spades. Of course you might open one spade!

Obviously if you are facing a passed hand you can afford to be less critical. One of the authors recently saw Andrew Robson open two diamonds holding:

    ♠ Q 7 3
    ♡ 9 3
    ◊ Q 10 9 7 6
    ♣ J 9 8

It is also the position where the bid may be made on a five-card suit, for example:

    ♠ 8
    ♡ 7 5 3
    ◊ K Q J 7 4
    ♣ K 8 4 2

would be a perfectly acceptable two diamonds.

Some players would regard the presence of the king of clubs in the previous example as something of a luxury! Take a look at this full deal from one of the North American Championships:

Dealer West. Love All.

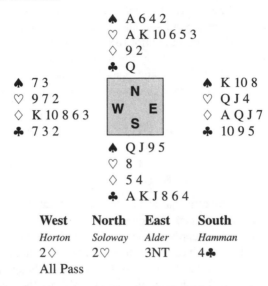

	♠ A 6 4 2		
	♡ A K 10 6 5 3		
	◇ 9 2		
	♣ Q		

♠ 7 3   ♠ K 10 8
♡ 9 7 2   ♡ Q J 4
◇ K 10 8 6 3   ◇ A Q J 7
♣ 7 3 2   ♣ 10 9 5

♠ Q J 9 5
♡ 8
◇ 5 4
♣ A K J 8 6 4

West	North	East	South
Horton	*Soloway*	*Alder*	*Hamman*
2◇	2♡	3NT	4♣
All Pass			

East might have paid a heavy price for his bold jump to three no-trumps, but combined with the pre-emptive opening, it actually caused our illustrious opponents to get their wires crossed and miss an easy game.

Responding to Weak Two Bids

When it comes to responding to a weak two bid, a reply of two no-trumps should be forcing, asking the opener to describe his hand. Before we explain how the opener should do that, there are some other situations that need to be considered. The first two are straightforward – raising partner with support. Two examples will suffice:

West	North	East	South
2♡	Pass	?	

(a) ♠ 7 3   (b) ♠ 8 5
    ♡ A J 10 6   ♡ J 9 4
    ◇ K 8 5 2   ◇ A Q 10 7 3
    ♣ 9 6 3   ♣ 7 4 2

On (a), you can pressurise your opponents by jumping to four hearts whilst on (b) you should simply raise to three hearts.

Don't forget the basic principles relating to responding to pre-emptive bids apply, so with a hand like:

♠ Q 7 4 2
♡ 5
◇ A K J 6
♣ K J 7 4

You should calmly pass your partner's opening bid of two hearts.

The next question is should a change of suit should be forcing? For example:

West	North	East	South
Pass	2♡	Pass	2♠
Pass	?		

We suggest that a new suit at the two level is regarded as constructive but not forcing. The opener should be prepared to raise with suitable non-minimum hands. If we consider this one:

♠ 7 5 3
♡ A 6 3
◇ Q 10 9 8 7 3
♣ 7

Then having opened two diamonds, opener would be happy to raise either major.

Using this hand as an example:

♠ J 8 7 4
♡ A Q J 8 5 3
◇ 8
♣ 4 2

If responder replies to an opening bid of two hearts with two spades then it would be in order to jump to four diamonds, a splinter bid, which we will be considering in more detail later on.

A new suit at the three level should be forcing and will not usually have much of a fit for the opener's suit – as you will see in a moment those hands are best dealt with by using the artificial response of two no-trumps.

This would be a typical hand:

West	North	East	South
2♡	Pass	?	

♠ A K Q J 7 3
♡ 6
♢ A 8 5
♣ Q J 7

East should bid three spades.

We mentioned earlier that a response of two no-trumps is forcing and asks the opener to describe his hand. There is no universally accepted way of replying but here is a set of responses that is based on the ones originally proposed by Harold Ogust, who represented America in two World Championships.

3♣   shows a bad hand and a bad suit
3♢   shows a good hand but a bad suit
3♡   shows a bad hand but a good suit
3♠   shows a good hand and a good suit
3NT   shows A-K-Q-x-x-x (!)

A response of three no-trumps is very rare and that bid might be better employed to show a maximum hand with a suit headed by two of the top three honours. For example: A-K-J-x-x-x, A-Q-J-x-x-x or A-K-10-9-x-x.

This is one of the areas in bidding where new ideas are still emerging – perhaps you will develop an idea that we can incorporate into the next edition!

Should you play weak twos?

To a certain extent it depends on your temperament. Certainly these bids have a greater frequency than Acol two bids. We like the suggestion made by the brilliant Sandra Landy: that weak twos are played in the first three positions, and Acol twos used fourth in hand.

Opening Pre-emptively At the Three Level

Let's consider some hands:

(a)	♠ K Q 10 9 7 6 3	(b)	♠ 9 8 7 6	(c)	♠ A K
	♡ 4		♡ A K 10 8 6 4 2		♡ 7 2
	◇ 9 7 3		◇ 8		◇ 7 4
	♣ 8 4		♣ 2		♣ 8 7 6 5 4 3 2

Hand (a) is a classic pre-emptive opening bid of three spades. You are pretty certain to get home with six tricks and you have absolutely no defence to opponents' heart, or any other game. Hand (b) looks very similar, but it would be quite wrong to open three hearts – just suppose partner had a good hand in spades! Unless he is really strong he will heed your warning not to disturb your hearts. Pass and await developments. With hand (c) you might feel a temptation to open three clubs, but temptation should be resisted! Your clubs are rotten, and no red-blooded opponent is going to be put off bidding over them anyway. Above all you have two defensive tricks, so pass and see what happens. By the way, we hope you've noticed that the old wives' tale about needing an outside ace is rubbish – if you added an ace to any of our three hands, it would be too strong for a pre-empt.

Responding to a Pre-emptive Opening at the Three Level

It's usually quite easy to recognise a good hand on which to open with a pre-emptive three-bid, but it's not always quite so easy to know what action to take when it's your partner, not you, who makes the pre-empt. We remember once asking a group of students, new to us but supposed to be quite experienced, what sort of responding hand would consider bidding three no-trumps in answer to partner's opening three, only to receive the answer in chorus 'Oh! You never disturb your partner's pre-empt, whatever you have!' Let's recap on the responses to opening three bids by looking at some possible hands for you to hold when your partner has opened, say, three hearts:

(a)	♠ A Q 7 4	(b)	♠ A Q 7 4	(c)	♠ J 9 8 7
	♡ J		♡ 10 9 8		♡ J 10 8 6 5 2
	◇ A K 6 3		◇ A J 10		◇ 4
	♣ K Q 9 8		♣ K Q 5		♣ 7 6

Do you think hand (a) is the perfect answer to the question we asked our group of students and just right for a response of three no-trumps? Of course you don't! Hand (b) is just what you want, however. You hold three cards in partner's suit, so can hardly imagine that you won't be able to clear it and run it, and you have a good holding in each of the other suits. With the lead coming up to your hand you'll be very unlucky not to make three no-trumps comfortably. So what is right on hand (a)? Surely you couldn't dream of not disturbing his three hearts with all those goodies! Why, four hearts of course! If you said that, this time you'll be right. It would be wrong to bid three no-trumps with only a singleton of partner's suit, because you'll probably be cut off from all his hearts – remember he won't have an outside entry – and you'll have to fall back on making eight or so tricks in your own hand. The defence will have to be very poor to let you do that! But the one thing partner won't need from you is trumps and you've plenty of outside tricks. Notice that in each of the two hands you could see at least three and a half to four tricks in your own hand, which should make partner's six to seven heart tricks up to a fair shot at game. When responding to a minor suit opening bid, and considering going to game, you'll need even more.

Is hand (c) an obvious 'no bid'? Well, if the player on your right passes the opening three hearts, stop to consider where all the points are. Three of you haven't got much, so the fourth player must be sitting there with a powerhouse and be just dying to get in his 'asking' call. Make life as difficult for him as you possibly can with a bid of five hearts or, if you feel brave enough, six hearts! You couldn't do that? Of course you could. What possible defence have you got to a slam in either minor? And if, refusing to be silenced, they go into spades, you might be a bit of a nuisance to them. No, naturally you don't expect to make the contract, and you'll probably be doubled, but the enemy has certainly got a game on somewhere, and probably a slam, so your 'advance sacrifice' will be well worthwhile.

Those were pretty obvious things to do in answer to partner's opening pre-empt. Let's now look at some not quite so obvious ones. Again, partner has started the auction with three hearts:

(a) ♠ A K Q J 9	(b) ♠ K 2	(c) ♠ K Q 8 7 6 5 2
♡ —	♡ A Q J 7	♡ —
◊ K J 6 2	◊ A K Q J 10 8	◊ 4 3 2
♣ K Q 7 5	♣ 7	♣ 5 4 3

Holding hand (a) bid three spades. This is forcing for one round and asks partner for more information about his hand. He certainly won't hold four spades for his pre-empt, but he may hold three, and as your bid shows a genuine spade suit and is a game force, he can bid the game in your suit instead of his, and as he certainly can't hold more than three minor suit cards, you can surely get in some ruffs in his hand. With hand (b) bid four diamonds. A change of suit from a major to a minor over a pre-empt is generally used as a slam try agreeing opener's suit (in this case hearts) as trumps, and asking for a black suit 'feature' such as an ace, a king, or a singleton or void. If partner cue bids either black suit you can bid six hearts with fair confidence, and if he just repeats hearts, you can pass. If you're wondering why you don't just use a Blackwood four no-trumps to get the information you require, consider how irritating it will be for partner, with no ace, to play in five hearts and lose the first three tricks. It's you he'll be irritated with, too!

Don't be tempted to bid holding hand (c). In other words, never 'rescue' into a suit which is possibly not as good as partners. If you do, disaster will surely follow, as partner will expect you to hold something like hand (a). Just pass. Yes, of course, it will be horrible for partner, but he's unlikely to be doubled at the three level, so he'll just go quietly down if the other side don't come in at the four level. There's no such bid as a pre-empt in response to a pre-empt.

We hope from this that you'll have realised the only truth about not disturbing partner's pre-empt is that you must hold your peace when you have an ordinary humdrum responding hand lacking three and a half or more quick tricks. Just hope that you haven't got enough to prevent the opposition from making a contract you've kept them out of bidding, or that what you have will help partner not to go too many down to be worthwhile.

Countering a Pre-emptive Opening at the Three Level

Now we want to say something about the action you can take when the player on your right has opened with a pre-emptive three bid. The first and most important thing is to have agreed beforehand with partner what your conventional defence is. All other calls then become natural. There are few things more trying than to bid what you think is a natural three Spades over a three heart opening, only to find that your partner thinks it's a take-out request. The second thing to appreciate, is that pre-empts are made with the express intention of embarrassing the opposition, and that sometimes you'll have to accept that you've been 'fixed'.

It simply isn't good enough, just because you have a hand with 13 points and a five-card suit on which you would certainly have opened the bidding, or intervened at the one level, to charge into the auction at the three level. Partner will play you for something better, and bid accordingly, and it will be your fault if you end up doubled and suffer a large penalty.

There are many defences, with which to compete against opening three bids, and it's a sure bet that, whichever one you and partner agree to play, when faced with the need to make it, you'll wish you'd agreed to play something else!

That's why opening pre-empts are such a useful offensive weapon. If you want to make a natural call in your own suit when you've got to come in at the three level, you need a good suit and depending on the vulnerability, hopes of six or seven tricks, even if partner holds a bust. Lacking a six-card suit you should probably use your agreed take-out request, and you generally need a hand of better than minimum opening values, to come into the bidding, that is, around 15 points.

The take-out double is by far and away the best defence to three-level pre-empts. It does not preclude the possibility of taking a penalty, as partner is free to pass with the right sort of defensive hand, and that means some decent trumps!

The best use for three no-trumps is as a natural bid. Of course, you need a reasonable hand and a stopper in the opponent's suit. Say the opening bid has been three spades. If you have a fair hand that includes ♠ A-x-x, then you will usually be able to ensure that the long spade suit is not threatening by holding up once or twice.

At rubber these days, if you have enough of the pre-emptor's suit to want to play in no-trumps, you have a hand on which to double for penalties. However, in duplicate bridge when you are the vulnerable pair, defeating their non-vulnerable contract, even by three tricks, won't be a good enough score if you could make game in no-trumps yourself.

9
More About Pre-emptive Bidding

Opening bids of Four Clubs/Four Diamonds and Five Clubs/Five Diamonds

To open with four clubs or four diamonds simply shows slightly greater length and strength in your chosen minor, as you are tempting the opposition to double you at the ten-trick level instead of nine. Similarly, to start with a bid of five clubs or five diamonds just means that you have an exceptionally distributional hand, perhaps 8-4, 7-5 or even 7-4 in the minors, or a nine, or ten card suit, and absolutely nothing in the major suits. Both bids are intended as advance sacrifices and you should be conscious of the vulnerability. Vulnerable opponents will hate to let you get away with a sacrifice when they might well have a game on, but if you are the vulnerable side, particularly when they are not, they will settle for a certain +500 or +800. Occasionally partner may have a couple of tricks which actually help you to make your contract, maybe even doubled, but really you are hoping to push the opponents in at the deep end when partner has a nasty surprise for them!

Hand (a) below is a typical opening of four diamonds and hand (b) would warrant a bid of five clubs.

(a) ♠ 8	(b) ♠ —
♡ 4 3	♡ 6
◇ K Q J 10 9 8 7 5	◇ K 2
♣ 8 2	♣ A K 10 9 8 7 6 5 3 2

Defending against these bids is maddening for the opposition. There are no artificial defences and bids are natural, a double being played as optional. Over an opening bid at the four level, four no-trumps can be used to show a two-suited hand.

Opening Bids of Four Hearts/Four Spades

An opening of four of a major is even more pre-emptive than an opening three. When made first or second in hand it has game possibilities and should be showing about eight playing tricks, with at least a seven card suit, but with next to no defence to a contract played anywhere but in the pre-emptor's suit. Partner is entitled to bid on if holding some outside values that will usually include at least two aces. If the opening is made third in hand after two passes, then it is accepted that partner will not bid on other than to continue the sacrifice.

Hand (a) is an excellent opening of four hearts in any position, and hand (b) should be opened with a bid of four spades.

(a) ♠ 8   (b) ♠ A K Q 9 8 7 6 3
    ♡ K Q 10 9 7 6 5 4   ♡ 8
    ◇ A 9 8   ◇ 7 4
    ♣ 9   ♣ 6 3

You are hoping that life has been made almost impossible for the enemy!

Responding to a Weak Four Bid

Since four spades and four hearts are game bids you should only disturb them if you are looking for a slam. You may want to raise an opening bid of four diamonds or four clubs to game if you have the right sort of hand. With a very good hand you will probably wish partner had not pre-empted but that's life. In the long run pre-empts will give you more gains than losses.

Opening Bids of Five Hearts and Five Spades

This is another rare bid and the opportunity to use it won't arise very often. However, it is the only bid which will extract from partner the exact information that you will need to determine the right contract. The bid describes an extremely powerful hand with eleven playing tricks, based on a long trump suit which lacks only the ace and king. Responder is required to pass with neither key card, to raise to six with either of them and, to seven if he should happen to have them both. Look at the following hand:

Opener	Responder	
♠ Q J 10 9 8 7 3 2	(a) ♠ 6 5	(b) ♠ A K
♡ —	♡ A K Q J 9	♡ 7 5 4 2
◇ A K	◇ Q J 10	◇ 8 4 3 2
♣ A K Q	♣ J 10 9 8	♣ 5 4 2

It's a wonderful hand but if partner holds hand (a) five spades is the optimum contract despite the combined count of 33 high-card points. Facing hand (b) partner's 7 points are exactly what you need, and the grand slam is 99.9% certain.

The 'Gambling' Three No-Trump Opening

From the opponents' point of view, an opening bid of three no-trumps is very obstructive. In first or second position, it is usually made on a solid seven-card minor suit with no more than a queen outside – what we call a 'running minor' and, as you see, virtually nothing else. Either of the two hands below would qualify:

(a) ♠ 7 3	(b) ♠ 9 6 5
♡ J 6 4	♡ 8 4 2
◇ A K Q J 9 6 4	◇ —
♣ 7	♣ A K Q J 10 6 3

Third in hand, you may well have one or more outside stoppers.

Responding to the 'Gambling' Three No-Trumps

It's an odd thing, but though pretty well all seasoned players know the three no-trumps opening, few of them know the best way to respond. Here are the responses:

Pass   prepared to play in three no-trumps.

4♣   not interested in three no-trumps, but prepared to play in four clubs or four diamonds, partner converting if his suit is diamonds.

4◇   an asking bid requesting opener to show a singleton or void.

4♡/4♠   to play

4NT   asks partner to convert to his suit at the five-level.

5♣/5◇   to play in five clubs or five diamonds, but note that in contrast to the four no-trump response, here the lead will come up to responder's hand.

If responder bids four diamonds to ask for a singleton or void, opener rebids as follows:

4♡	a singleton or void heart.
4♠	a singleton or void spade.
4NT	no singleton or void.
5♣	a singleton or void *diamond*.
5♢	a singleton or void *club*.

Let's look at a few hands on which, in the light of the above rules for responding, you should know what to do. Partner has opened three no-trumps and you hold:

(a) ♠ A J 7 2	(b) ♠ 7	(c) ♠ 9 7 6 4 3	(d) ♠ A 7 6 4 2
♡ J 4 3	♡ K 8 4 3	♡ A K Q J	♡ A K Q 5
♢ A 10 6 5 4	♢ 8 7	♢ A 8	♢ 8 6
♣ 6	♣ A K Q J 6 5	♣ 7 3	♣ 7 5

With hand (a) you know for certain that partner's suit is clubs – he can't have a 'running' diamond suit whilst you have the ace of diamonds. Pass, because your best chance of making game is to play three no-trumps, the only danger being a heart lead. With (b) you're in no doubt at all that partner's suit is diamonds. Bid a direct five diamonds, as clearly as it will be better if the opening lead comes up to your hand. With hand (c) you want to be in at least five clubs (clearly partner's suit), but a slam is likely to be available if partner holds a void or singleton spade. Make the singleton asking bid of four diamonds and if the response is four spades you can bid six clubs. If partner denies a singleton spade, five clubs will be enough. On hand (d) you can't tell whether partner has diamonds or clubs, but you do know you've got enough to want him to play in game in his suit, whichever it is, so bid four no-trumps, and he will convert to five of the minor he holds.

Opening Bid of Four No-Trumps

This is another rare bid but when it does turn up you want to be sure that partner understands that you are not making a simple Blackwood enquiry. You want more specific information out of him than just how many aces he holds. Look at the two hands below:

(a) ♠ K Q J 10 8 2   (b) ♠ A K Q J
  ♡ A K Q   ♡ A K Q J 10 9
  ◇ —   ◇ K Q J
  ♣ A K Q J   ♣ —

With hand (a) if partner has one ace you will make a small slam, but to bid a grand slam you need him specifically to hold the ace of spades – the ace of diamonds would be waste paper. If you plough through a 'Blackwood' sequence and find he has one ace, you won't know which one it is, so you'll have to stop in six spades or take a flyer if you decide to bid seven. Don't risk it – open four no-trumps, to which partner responds as follows:

5♣	With no ace
5◇/5♡/5♠	With the ◇A, ♡A or ♠A
6♣	With the ♣A
5NT	With two aces

So if the incredible turns up and he bids five spades you can bid the grand slam. If he shows the ace of diamonds with five diamonds, or no ace, then settle for six spades, in the latter case hoping partner can take care of the third round of hearts.

Hand (b) is another typical example. The ace of clubs would be worthless, the ace of diamonds gold dust. Open four no-trumps, and if partner responds five or six clubs bid six hearts. If he responds five diamonds, go to seven hearts.

Pre-emptive Jump Raises of Partner's Opening Bid

We can't leave the subject of pre-emptive bidding without considering that although the majority of pre-emptive bids are made by opener, pre-empts can be a valuable weapon in the hands of both responder and overcaller. Pre-empting your partner by leaping sky-high in a suit of your own when he has already opened at the one level is very rarely right, but to pre-empt the opposition on weakness when you have a splendid fit with partner is a very good idea. It is best made at favourable or equal vulnerability, the idea being to make it difficult for your opponents to reach their best spot.

Here are some responder's hands for you to look at:

(a) ♠ 7   (b) ♠ A K 5   (c) ♠ 8 4
  ♡ Q 9 7 5 2   ♡ Q 9 7 5   ♡ 9
  ◇ K J 8 6 2   ◇ K 10 9 8 ◇ K Q 9 7 5 3
  ♣ 8 4   ♣ 9 4   ♣ J 10 9 7

Holding hand (a) you hear partner open with one heart and your right-hand opponent passes. Jump at once to four hearts in an effort to shut out your left-hand opponent. Partner might be weak, we hear you say, and we might go down! (doubled even!) So what? If you only bid two hearts there is every chance that the next player will be able to get involved. There are plenty of hands partner can have where he will be able to make the contract.

Holding hand (b) the last thing you want is to leap straight up to game when partner opens one heart. Yes, you know you'll never let him play lower than four hearts, but you must start a delayed game raise sequence by bidding two diamonds and await his rebid. You do not fear intervention from the other side.

Hand (c) is more complex. If partner starts with one diamond, you could jump to some number of diamonds at once, especially if there has been an intervening bid on your right. However, if partner has a strong balanced hand, you may have missed three no-trumps. On balance, we think it is best not to worry too much about that and just raise the ante in diamonds. We are still debating whether four or five diamonds is correct!

Pre-emptive Jump Overcalls

The right type of hand on which to make a pre-emptive jump intervening bid is that with which you are sitting waiting for your right-hand opponent to pass so that you can open with a weak three level or higher bid.

Look back earlier in this chapter and the preceding one and you will see some excellent examples of hands which could be used as intervening bids instead of as opening bids.

Just be very sure that at whatever level you make your overcall, you have missed out at least two levels at which you could have bid your suit. Otherwise you will be telling partner that you have a good hand with playing strength, and you might well come to grief with the final contract.

If the player on your right opens one club or one diamond, a jump to three hearts by you would show this type of hand.

However, if the opening bid is one spade, then a jump to three hearts would be strong. The thing to remember is that if the opener's bid was in a suit lower-ranked than yours, then a jump to the three level will do, but if his suit is higher ranked than yours, then you will have to bid at least to the four level.

10
Fourth Suit Forcing

By now you will have learned a good deal about responder's rebids. If you use your Acol limit bids and preference bids correctly, you will have found that on most hands you, as responder, will have obvious bids to make. However, there are certain types of hands where you will not be sure of the best contract to play in, and to help you decide, you want more information from your partner. Usually this is because you feel that the best contract will be in no-trumps, but that to bid this yourself will be asking for trouble, as you have one rather weak suit and fear that partner, too, may be weak in the same suit.

Fourth Suit Forcing Convention

This is the time when you will find the 'fourth suit forcing' convention so useful. Here is a typical sequence:

$$1\heartsuit \quad 1\spadesuit$$
$$2\clubsuit \quad 2\diamondsuit$$

The bid of two diamonds is a bid of the fourth, hitherto unbid, suit in the auction. It doesn't mean that you, as responder, are two-suited in spades and diamonds. If you think about it, what a waste of time it would be for you to bid spades and diamonds, whilst you partner is bidding hearts and clubs! If you have got a reasonable holding in diamonds, you could perfectly well bid no-trumps yourself, either two or three no-trumps according to your strength. So a bid of the fourth suit asks partner to carry on describing their hand.

Here is your hand in the auction we mentioned earlier:

♠ A Q 9 7 2
♡ K 8
◇ 9 7 5
♣ A 7 4

Partner opened one heart, you replied one spade, he rebid two clubs, and you simply don't know what to do for the best. You have 13 points, and an opening bid facing an opening bid should produce a game somewhere. The question is, what game? Bid a 'fourth suit forcing' two diamonds and wait for more information. Partner will understand that he is being asked to go into no-trumps if he has stop in diamonds, and to make any other bid to clarify his hand if he can't help with the diamonds. Don't be afraid that you'll be left to play in two diamonds! Remember the title of this convention, 'fourth suit forcing'. Your two diamond bid doesn't promise a diamond suit, but it does demand that your partner should make at least one further bid. If he bids two no-trumps you will now confidently raise to three no-trumps. If he denies any help with diamonds by repeating his hearts, you can now happily bid the heart game and if instead he should give you delayed support for spades (showing three of them, not four) you will choose the spade game.

Here are some more hands on which the correct use of this convention will help you to get to the right contract, not merely guess at it:

(a) ♠ 10 9 7	(b) ♠ J 7	(c) ♠ Q 10 7 4
♡ K 8 6	♡ A J 10 7	♡ 9 8
◇ A Q 10 7 6	◇ 8 4	◇ K J 10 7 5
♣ A 7	♣ A K 10 7 4	♣ 6 2

On hand (a) you have replied one diamond to partner's opening one club. When he now rebids one heart you make a 'fourth suit forcing' rebid of one spade, hoping that he has something in spades and can, therefore, rebid in no-trumps. If he bids two no-trumps you will raise to game.

Note the difference on hand (b). Partner opens one spade and you respond two clubs. He now bids two diamonds. Don't ask him about hearts by bidding two hearts – you know you have the fourth suit well stopped. Tell him so by rebidding three no-trumps.

Hand (c) is rather different. Partner opens one club, and you respond one diamond. When partner now bids one heart, you don't have the values to bid the fourth suit. You would need at least 10 or 11 points, so you must bid one no-trump, telling partner you have a spade stopper and a minimum hand.

A bid of the fourth suit at the one- or two-level does not force the partnership to game, and the auction may be dropped when the best part-score is found. However, if you bid the fourth suit at the three-level and your partner has a stopper in the fourth suit, then he is going to bid three no-trumps. For practical purposes therefore, fourth suit forcing at the three level is forcing to game.

Remember:

1   **A bid of the fourth suit is unconditionally forcing for one round.**

2   **Don't use 'fourth suit forcing' if your hand contains a sensible natural call, such as a bid in no-trumps yourself.**

From Opener's Point of View

Now we must move over to the other side of the table and think what sort of bid you are going to make when faced with a 'fourth suit forcing' bid from responder. Here are three hands, on all of which you would open one spade:

(a) ♠ K Q 7 5 4	(b) ♠ A K Q 9 8	(c) ♠ K Q 10 9 5
♡ Q 10 8	♡ 10 2	♡ A Q 9 8 2
◇ A J 10 7	◇ A 10 9 7 5	◇ J 10 7
♣ 4	♣ 9	♣ —

On hand (a) when partner responds two clubs you would rebid two diamonds, and he now bids two hearts. You should be happy to show your good hold on the heart suit by bidding two no-trumps. With more than a minimum opening you should bid three no-trumps.

On hand (b) after the same first four bids, you must deny any help in hearts and, tell your partner you have a rebiddable diamond suit by saying three diamonds.

With hand (c) you have no possible interest in a no-trump contract. You would, of course, have rebid two hearts over partner's two clubs, not two diamonds as in hands (a) and (b), so the auction will have gone 1♠ – 2♣ – 2♡ – 3◇. Remember your partner is only asking about diamonds, not showing a diamond suit, but having bid the fourth suit at the three-level, your side is committed to game. Again, show your shape by rebidding three hearts and leave him to do the rest.

So you see how useful this 'fourth suit forcing' bid can be when, as responder, you are stuck for a sensible rebid. It can save you from many a disastrous shot at three no-trumps when you hold no better than Q-x in a suit and find partner with only a losing doubleton himself.

11
Directional Asking Bids

This is another weapon to be added to your armoury, and it falls into place here, as it is another way of investigating for a safe no-trump contract rather than just guessing. A Directional Asking Bid, known as a DAB, is often the only way in which a partnership can reach a no-trump contract, though this time in the face of an opponent's opening or intervening bid.

There are many hands (you must have met some of them already) which you feel you would like to play in no-trumps except for a weakness in the suit bid by your opponents. You could just close your eyes and 'shoot' three no-trumps, hoping for the best, but you can improve on that. All you have to do is find out whether your partner can supply a stopper in the suit that has been bid against you. In much the same way as you asked about a missing suit by using a 'fourth suit forcing' bid, now you ask about a suit bid by your opponents. Let's go into this more fully, so that you get the idea:

(a) ♠ Q J 8	(b) ♠ J 8	(c) ♠ Q J
♡ K J 6	♡ K J 5	♡ A J 9
◇ A K J 5	◇ A K J 10 4	◇ A 9 4
♣ A 7 3	♣ A 7 2	♣ K Q J 9 4

On hand (a) you open the obvious one diamond to which partner responds two clubs. 'Lovely,' you think, and are just going to open your mouth to bid a direct three no-trumps when your right-hand opponent sticks in a bid of two spades. You are, of course, going to refuse to be put off because your own spades constitute a certain stop, and you're going to bid your three no-trumps regardless.

Hand (b) is a different story. You open one diamond and partner responds two clubs. Again your right-hand opponent comes in with two spades. How very irritating of him! It's now a racing certainty that your left-hand opponent will lead a spade, and if partner has nothing in the suit, that will defeat three no-trumps before you even get off the ground. Yet if partner has as little as ♠ Q-x-x there is a good chance that three no-trumps will make when five of a minor will be too many. How can you find out whether partner has a little something in spades?

The answer is simple if you know your DABs – ask him! No, you aren't allowed to say 'partner, have you a partial stop in spades?' but you are allowed to make a DAB, a cue-bid in spades. Here your DAB will be a bid of three spades. If partner can't help with the opponent's suit, again he makes any other bid his hand warrants.

One point to watch is the level at which you make this bid. Hand (b) was very strong and you didn't mind forcing partner to rebid at the four-level if he couldn't find a three no-trumps call, which would show his partial stop in spades. Had the auction been (on a weaker hand, of course) one club from you, one diamond from your partner, and one heart or one spade from your right-hand opponent, you would have been able to make your DAB at the two-level. That would not require such a high point count, as if partner cannot bid two no-trumps, he will be able to bid a minor at the three level, and that is a bid you would be allowed to pass.

Now let's turn to hand (c). Another use for the DAB is to ensure that the no-trump contract is played by the hand more likely to make it. If your right-hand opponent has bid a suit, it may be to your advantage to get partner to bid and play the no-trump contract. This may sometimes result in the gain of a tempo and a trick. This is because your right-hand opponent, who bid the suit, will be on lead, and either he must open up his own suit, or he must lead another suit which will usually help your side.

Hand (c) is a case in point. You open one club and partner responds one diamond. Two no-trumps is your obvious rebid, but before you can make it your right-hand opponent overcalls with one spade. Now you need to find partner with something in spades. Try a DAB of two spades. If partner can bid two no-trumps you will have an easy raise to game. If partner's spade holding is ♠ A-5, a spade lead will cost the defenders a potentially important trick.

We have so far considered a DAB as coming after your opening bid and partner's response, and an intervention by your right-hand opponent. It is true that this is the most usual occasion for its use, but it can come at any time. Partner opens one spade and is overcalled with two hearts.

(a) ♠ K 3 2   (b) ♠ K 3
    ♡ J 4   ♡ A 9 4
    ◇ A 9 7 4   ◇ Q 9 7 4
    ♣ K J 8 2   ♣ K J 8 2

On hand (a) or (b) bid three hearts. Partner should respond on the assumption that this is a DAB, but if you happen to have made the bid (are there enough points in the pack?) to mean it as showing a rock-crusher with first round control of hearts, you can put the record straight on the next round. Holding either hand (a) or (b) bid three hearts. Partner will respond to your DAB and you will discover whether or not the right spot for your contract is three no-trumps.

An alternative way to treat these hands is explained in Chapter 17, where we introduce you to the Negative Double.

Just occasionally a bid that sounds like a DAB was just a waiting bid from opener to force more information from his partner. Look at the hands below:

Opener	Responder	
♠ A 4	(a) ♠ Q 7 2	(b) ♠ Q 7 2
♡ A K Q 7 6	♡ J 3	♡ J 3
◇ Q 10 4 3	◇ A K 9 8 4	◇ A K 9 8 5 2
♣ Q J	♣ K 10 9	♣ 9 8

Over the bid of one heart there is an overcall of one spade and on each of the responding hands responder bids two diamonds which passes round to opener whose best bid now is two spades. Again both responding hands merit a bid of two no-trumps to show the spade half-stop. However, when the opener now bids three diamonds his call of two spades can now be understood to be the first move on a good hand in support of diamonds, with some slam potential. With hand (a) responder can confidently co-operate by cue bidding the king of clubs, whereas with hand (b) he can do no more than bid five diamonds. Note that had opener plunged straight into Blackwood after the initial response of two diamonds, he would not have known, over the five diamond reply, whether or not to attempt the slam.

Remember:

A Directional Asking Bid (DAB) is nearly always a bid in the opponent's suit which asks partner whether he can provide a stopper in the suit to make a no-trump contract a safe proposition rather than a wild guess.

12
Trial Bidding

Long Suit Trial Bids After Major Suit Agreement

In the early days of bridge, if your partner opened one of a major and all you could do was give a single raise, you had three options. You could pass, go directly to game, or make an unscientific raise to the three level, asking partner if his hand was minimum or maximum.

It was quickly realised that there are better ways of dealing with this situation. To begin with, a raise by opener to three of either major, is used pre-emptively to prevent the opposition from re-opening the auction.

If the opening bidder is not strong enough bid game on his own, but thinks one might be possible if the responder has a good raise to the two-level, he can make a *trial bid*. There are several variations in use, but we think the simplest method is to bid the suit in which you need some help. This could be a genuine second suit, or it may be a poor three card holding, sometimes even three small cards. That is known as a long suit trial bid.

An alternative is to make your trial bid on a shortage, usually a doubleton or singleton – a short suit trial bid. A partnership must know, and state, whether it employs long or short suit trial bids. Any form of trial bid is, unconditionally forcing for one round. It has been agreed that the partnership will play in their major suit fit, and it is merely a question of whether it will be at game level. Opener guarantees that his major suit is five cards in length when he rebids another suit at the three level. If his longest suit were only four cards in length he would have a balanced hand and he would have opened or rebid in no-trumps.

From the simple fact that opener doesn't pass the two-level raise, he is known to be better than minimum. In fact he must be reasonably good, because he already knows from the single raise that responder is limited to nine points and a four-card trump fit. Look at the following example:

Opener	Responder	
♠ K Q J 9 6 4	(a) ♠ A 7 5 3	(b) ♠ A 7 5 3
♡ 7	♡ J 10 8	♡ Q J 8 7
◇ A J 9	◇ 6 3	◇ 10 3
♣ K 8 4	♣ Q J 7 2	♣ 7 6 2

You open one spade, and game is almost certain to be made if your partner holds the first hand, and almost equally certain to fail if he holds the second. You could pass or take a flyer at four spades, but finishing in the right spot will be a matter of luck. This is not so if you select clubs as the suit in which you need help, and bid three clubs. The following are responder's replies.

Responding to the Trial Bid

1 On a minimum hand, wherever his values, responder should convert to opener's suit at the lowest available level.

2 On a maximum, or near maximum hand for the two-level raise, he should convert to opener's suit at game level.

3 If doubtful, he should let his holding in the suit in which opener has made his trial bid decide the issue, bidding at the three-level if he lacks 'help' in the trial-bid suit and going to game if he holds help.

Applying these guidelines to our original example, responder is maximum for his raise of one spade to two spades. When opener trial-bids three clubs, go straight to four spades. On the second hand, though technically 'maximum', it's a poor hand for anyone wanting to play in four spades, and asking for help in clubs so just convert to three spades.

Here are three hands which you, as responder, might hold when partner has opened one spade and you have raised him to two spades.

(a) ♠ K 9 6 4	(b) ♠ Q 8 5 4	(c) ♠ K 4 3 2
♡ 3	♡ 9 7	♡ K Q
◇ A 9 5 4	◇ K Q 4 2	◇ 7 5 4 2
♣ 9 7 4 3	♣ 10 5 3	♣ 5 3 2

Holding hand (a) raise partner to four spades no matter which suit he makes the trial bid in. Heart losers can be ruffed in dummy and a holding of either minor facing your four-card length should allow declarer to develop ten tricks. With hand (b) a trial bid in hearts or clubs from opener does not improve your hand and you should sign off with three spades. If the trial bid is in diamonds, jump to four Spades. Hand (c) looks quite attractive but no matter what the trial bid is made in, sign off at the three level. The doubleton ♡ K-Q will not play its full value, even if partner's try is in hearts. There will be too many minor suit losers. Remember that the point count for opener's bid is around the 17 point mark. With a stronger hand he would have bid the game outright.

Trial Bids After Minor Suit Agreement

Trial bids after responder has raised opener's one club or one diamond are played quite differently from trial bids after major suit agreement. They are directed almost invariably to exploring for the easier game in no-trumps. Opener guarantees a hold on the suit he bids and by inference declares a weakness in another suit, which he hopes responder can stop. After a single raise it is rare for opener still to be trying for three no-trumps but take the following hand:

♠ A 9 2
♡ 6
♢ K Q J 10 9 5
♣ A J 10

Responder raises your opening one diamond to two diamonds and you don't need much imagination to see that if he holds the ace of diamonds the suit is good for six tricks. You have the two black aces, but are still a long way from eleven tricks. On the other hand, three no-trumps, with that singleton heart, looks equally fraught with danger. Now, however, you have the means to ask partner whether he has a stop in hearts. Make a trial bid of three clubs and, if he shows a heart stop by bidding three hearts, you can bid three no-trumps. It may be even better to bid three spades, allowing partner to bid no-trumps, but you need to be on the same wavelength! If he skips hearts and shows a spade stop with three spades you can go back to diamonds.

When the bidding starts 1♣ – 3♣ or 1♢ – 3♢ and opener has a reasonably balanced hand of about 15–16 points, the partnership needs to explore the possibilities for playing in three no-trumps before committing themselves to a part-score or game in a minor suit. Look at these hands:

(a)

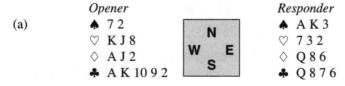

	Opener		Responder
	♠ 7 2		♠ A K 3
	♡ K J 8		♡ 7 3 2
	♢ A J 2		♢ Q 8 6
	♣ A K 10 9 2		♣ Q 8 7 6

The opening bid of one club is raised to three clubs. If responder can stop the spade suit, then three no-trumps ought to be a fine contract. So opener now bids three diamonds and receives the reply of three spades, which is all he needs to bid three no-trumps.

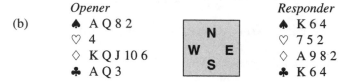

(b)

Opener	Responder
♠ A Q 8 2	♠ K 6 4
♡ 4	♡ 7 5 2
◇ K Q J 10 6	◇ A 9 8 2
♣ A Q 3	♣ K 6 4

The bidding goes 1◇ – 3◇ and opener's rebid of Three Spades invites partner to try three no-trumps holding a stop in hearts. He can't provide a stopper, but with such prime cards he can afford to show his second round control in clubs by bidding four clubs. If there is now an exchange of cue bids, with four hearts and four spades, then it will be easy for the opener to bid the small slam in diamonds.

A Try for No-Trumps After Major Suit Agreement

Sometimes even after a 4-4 major suit fit has been discovered it may be better for the contract to be played in no-trumps because of the balanced nature of the two hands. If the bidding proceeds: 1♠ – 2♠ – 2NT, opener is showing a balanced hand of 16–17 points and denying a five-card spade suit. (An auction of 1♠ – 2♠ – 3NT would promise 18–19 points.) Responder is asked to choose between four possible replies.

He can retreat to three spades, showing an unbalanced hand of minimal value but with ruffing power, or can raise to four spades to show greater values again with ruffing power. Alternatively he can pass two no-trumps with 6–7 high-card points or raise to three no-trumps with 8–9 points. Both bids deny a shapely hand where trumps can be used to advantage. A couple of examples will help.

(a)

Opener	Responder
♠ A Q 10	♠ J 4 2
♡ K J 10 9	♡ A 7 6 4
◇ Q J 10	◇ 6 5 3
♣ K 7 5	♣ A 8 4

With the pair of hands in (a) the bidding should go 1♡ – 2♡ – 2NT – 3NT for with two perfectly balanced hands nine tricks will be easier than ten.

(b)

Opener		Responder
♠ A K 4 2		♠ Q J 9 8 3
♡ K J 9	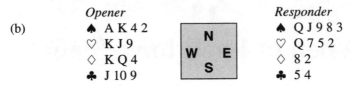	♡ Q 7 5 2
◇ K Q 4		◇ 8 2
♣ J 10 9		♣ 5 4

In example (b) the bidding will start 1♠ – 2♠ – 2NT and responder will correct to three spades. Note that opener must respect responder's decision and resist the temptation to raise to four spades!

13
When to Look for a Slam

Unless you're a very lucky card holder, it won't be more than once, perhaps, in an evening that you'll pick up a simply super hand, and think at once that game must be certain and slam possible if partner has anything at all. Yet so often the slam is missed when it was lay-down, and just as often a partnership bids itself into a silly slam which was going down from the moment the opening lead was made. So this is a good moment to point out something that should be obvious, but which so many players never seem to grasp. Every time you bid an unmakeable slam, not only do you not gain the slam bonus on top of the game you obviously had, you also lose that certain game.

If you were vulnerable at the time you overbid, you have just lost a valuable game bonus. So now we're going to give you some guidance as to when to think about bidding a slam.

The first important thing to learn is that slams in no-trumps, with two balanced hands facing each other, shouldn't be bid without 33–34 high card points for a small slam and 37+ for a grand slam. When neither hand contains a five-card nor longer suit it can be hard work making the required number of tricks, even when you have plenty of points. It's no good being able to win twelve tricks after the opponents have cashed a couple of aces, but you will realise that providing you hold 33 high-card points between you, you can't be missing more than one ace! The same principles apply, for the grand slam needing 37 points.

Slams, either grand or small, in a trump contract, depend on the fit between the combined hands and on controls, and high card points play a less important part. We're sure that some time or another you have all had the experience of stopping in a part-score or game, and finding the hand is a lay-down for all thirteen tricks. We're not saying that all these slams can be bid, but certainly some of them can. Here is an example from a recent tournament.

Dealer South. North-South Game.

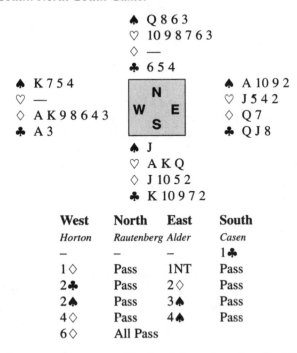

	♠ Q 8 6 3		
	♡ 10 9 8 7 6 3		
	◇ —		
	♣ 6 5 4		

♠ K 7 5 4   N   ♠ A 10 9 2
♡ —   W   E   ♡ J 5 4 2
◇ A K 9 8 6 4 3   S   ◇ Q 7
♣ A 3   ♣ Q J 8

♠ J
♡ A K Q
◇ J 10 5 2
♣ K 10 9 7 2

West	North	East	South
Horton	*Rautenberg*	*Alder*	*Casen*
–	–	–	1♣
1◇	Pass	1NT	Pass
2♣	Pass	2◇	Pass
2♠	Pass	3♠	Pass
4◇	Pass	4♠	Pass
6◇	All Pass		

East was known to have something in clubs and spades, almost certainly a doubleton diamond, and nothing wasted in hearts. That made six diamonds a reasonable bet. North led a heart, and after that was ruffed, a diamond to the queen revealed that South had a trump trick. Still, declarer had a string to his bow. The club finesse was right, and when the jack of spades appeared on the first round of the suit, it was not hard to finesse against North's queen.

The second important thing is not to rush the bidding at an early stage. Have you ever bid four no-trumps over partner's one of a suit, just because you held 16 high-card points and a bit of a fit with his suit? Only to realise that after the response an ace is missing, and that you haven't the faintest idea of whether to bid a slam or sign off at the five-level? You may even be too high immediately you bid that excitable four no-trumps!

Having told you what not to do, let's go on to consider some of the times when you should become slam-minded, the first and most obvious being when your partner bids two clubs and you have a positive response. Do listen to his rebids, though, before you insist on bidding beyond game.

(a) ♠ 8 4
   ♡ A K J 3 2
   ◇ 9 8 7
   ♣ 5 3 2

(b) ♠ K 6 3 2
   ♡ Q 7 4
   ◇ Q 9 7 2
   ♣ A 3

(c) ♠ K Q 9 7 2
   ♡ K Q J 2
   ◇ 8 2
   ♣ 7 2

On hand (a) you have just enough to make a positive response of two hearts to two clubs. If opener rebids two no-trumps, do your arithmetic, and work out that unless partner has extra values, your 8 points will only make a slam marginal. Therefore, just raise quietly to three no-trumps. If you are opener with a 23–24 point hand you, too, must be content with three no-trumps. You have said it all, and it is up to responder to make a slam try if there is to be one after your rebid. In the same way, going back to you in responder's seat, if opener rebids in a suit of his own, just rebid your hearts. Move one of the little minor suit cards up into spades, and if the rebid is two spades you can raise to three spades. Opener has guaranteed a five-card spade suit by his rebid for with a balanced hand he would have gone into no-trumps.

Hand (b) is a really nice sight if your partner opens two clubs, and the most descriptive response is two no-trumps showing a balanced hand with at least 8 points, and no good suit. Do not offer your spades as trumps. You will hate it if partner puts you into a spade slam and produces ♠ A-9-8-4 as trump support. You will have only yourself to blame, however, as to bid a major suit directly in answer to an opening two club bid guarantees a suit of at least five cards. You certainly intend to be in a slam somewhere but with a hand like (b) above make the limit bid and leave the rest to partner.

With hand (c), again you are sure you want to get to a slam somewhere, almost certainly in one of the majors. You should respond to two clubs with two spades and show the hearts on your next turn to bid if partner has shown no enthusiasm for your spades. If opener rebids three hearts over your two spades don't make the mistake of bidding a mere four hearts which opener might pass! Bid a direct four no-trumps – you know where you're going, and so will partner when you make this inferential agreement of his suit. The same, of course, applies if opener raises your initial two spades to three spades. In either case the only question now is whether you are going for a small slam or a grand slam. You can't bid four no-trumps without an ace in your hand? Of course you can! Either partner can initiate a 'Blackwood' slam investigation if it seems the right moment to do it, and think how many other high-card points partner must have if he can open two clubs missing what you've got.

Responder Jumps in a New Suit

It used to be common practice that when responder held 16 points (or in some schools just an opening bid) he should jump the bidding in a new suit, regardless of where his values lay. Modern theory says that unless responder is perfectly sure he knows which slam he pictures the partnership playing in he should go slowly, giving maximum room for investigation. A jump bid into a new suit by responder, therefore, shows either a six-card or longer solid or almost solid suit of his own, or a very good fit for opener's suit to which he will return at a later point in the bidding.

A jump bid followed by three no-trumps can be used to show 16–18 points with a 5-3-3-2 distribution, the doubleton usually being in partner's suit, especially if he has rebid it.

Here are three nice hands which responder might hold:

(a) ♠ 8 7	(b) ♠ A K Q J 6 5	(c) ♠ 2
♡ K Q 6 5	♡ 8 5 3	♡ A K 8 6 3
◇ 4	◇ J	◇ A K 9 6 5
♣ A K Q 9 6 2	♣ K Q 5	♣ K 9

Holding hand (a) if partner opens one heart, force with an immediate three clubs. Opener does not need much for a slam to be on. If the opening had been one spade or one diamond, bid a simple two clubs preparing to reverse into hearts. On hand (b) force with two spades no matter what suit partner opens. You intend to play in no less than four spades and are interested in going higher unless partner only has diamonds. With hand (c) over an opening bid of one spade, bid a quiet two hearts, planning to introduce diamonds on the next round. Over one club similarly bid one heart and await partner's rebid. Of course, if partner had opened with either red suit, jump in the other at once.

Never Forget:

1 **Don't bid your hand twice. This means that if you have forced on a minimum holding for your bid, don't be the one to go pressing on for a slam. You have told partner you've got a good hand – let him take it from there.**

2 **The dangers of 'Blackwood' in the minors. Slam investigations will probably have to be by way of cue bids, not 'Blackwood'.**

Frequently, of course, it will be opener who has visions of a slam as soon as he hears a strong reply from partner.

(a) ♠ A K 8 5 2	(b) ♠ A Q 7 3	(c) ♠ A Q 2
♡ A 5	♡ A K 8 5 2	♡ A K 8 5 3
◇ A Q 7 3	◇ A 2	◇ A Q J 9
♣ 9 2	♣ 9 2	♣ 2

On hand (a) you open one spade and partner forces with three clubs saying game is certain, slam possible, and you really must go along with the latter idea. Don't make the error of rebidding your spades in the mistaken belief that it's important to show a five-card suit. Bid three diamonds, waiting to hear partner's next bid. If he now returns to your spades, you are well towards bidding a slam, knowing the most suitable spot for it.

Holding hand (b) you open with one heart, intending to reverse into two spades when, much to your surprise, your partner forces with two spades. Don't jump to four spades, which would be a limit bid and a sign-off that might well be passed. Take it slowly. Bid three spades, agreeing the suit and leaving all the bidding space in the world for partner to make a cue bid or an ace-ask, if he wants to. If all he does is bid four spades, you know now that he has bid his hand to the limit and sensibly doesn't propose to bid it twice. You are the one who knows there must be a small slam on and that it's up to you to start slam investigations. Had your partner forced with three of a minor originally, not two spades, you would have reversed into three spades yourself, and left the next step to him.

Hand (c) contains 20 high-card points, but don't make the mistake of opening two no-trumps when you have a singleton! Start with a quiet one heart, intending to force with three diamonds over any response. Suppose, though, that over one heart partner forces with three clubs. The knowledge that partner has at least 16 points means that a slam must be certain. We would go on with three diamonds, allowing room to investigate the possibility of a grand slam.

Sometimes slams are missed because one of the players doesn't re-evaluate his hand when he hears an unexpected bid from partner. Look at these two hands opposite each other and examine the correct bidding sequence.

Opener		*Responder*
♠ A J 8 6		♠ K Q 9 7
♡ 4 2	N W E S	♡ A K 9 7 3
◇ A 7		◇ K 8
♣ A Q 8 7 5		♣ 6 4

The bidding proceeds: 1♣ – 1♡ – 1♠ – 4♠. Now it's up to opener not just to pass his partner's rebid of four spades, feeling pleased that game has been reached so easily even though he had only 15 points. He should listen to the message being sent across the table. Although partner could not force on his first response, over a simple rebid of one spade which might contain only 12 or so points, he bid an immediate game. Opener should look carefully at his ace of diamonds – his opening and rebid would be perfectly good without that valuable card, which his partner can't picture him as holding. So he should make a slam try enabling six spades to be reached with ease.

Think about a slam when:

1   One player opens two clubs and the other makes a positive response.

2   You open with an above minimum hand and partner jumps in a new suit.

3   Your partner opens, you yourself have a hand on which you were going to open the bidding, and then partner makes a jump rebid.

4   At any stage of the auction your partner raises to game and you have a far better hand than he can possibly picture.

Finally, remember that successful slam bidding is a matter of partnership trust and understanding. You must be able to rely on partner to force when he should, and to have the appropriate values. You must trust partner's strong bids, and re-evaluate your hand in the light of what he has said. Above all, you must be able to trust partner to honour a forcing bid and to keep the bidding open for you, so that you can afford to go slowly when you need time to make your investigation.

14
More About Bidding Slams

In the previous chapter we told you some of the situations which should make you investigate for a possible slam. Next we want to tell you about some of the conventional bids which will help you to choose the right slam, and find out in time if you really should be bidding it at all!

A frequent error is a player's assessment of what constitutes a Two Club opening bid. A balanced hand must contain 23 high-card points to be worth the bid, but a hand of powerful playing strength with one or more long suits, and holding five quick tricks, should also be described by our 'big bid' even if it does not contain 23 points. Accurate description of your hand is the keynote to arriving at the correct contract, so let's look at three hands on which you, as responder, must pick the right conventional reply to whichever strong two-level opening bid has been chosen by your partner.

(a) ♠ 10 4 2	(b) ♠ J 8 5 2	(c) ♠ 4 3
♡ 4 3	♡ J 4 3 2	♡ K 7 4 2
◇ A Q 7 4 2	◇ J 2	◇ A Q J 6 4
♣ 8 5 2	♣ K Q 4	♣ 7 5

The three strong opening bids we are considering are two no-trumps, an Acol strong two, and two clubs, and with hand (a) you have a different answer to each. Suppose partner opens two clubs – you haven't got the values necessary for a positive response so must bid the negative two diamonds. Had the opening been two no-trumps, then with a five-card suit and 6 points you are amply good enough to raise to three no-trumps. Had partner, instead, opened two spades you could respond three spades, showing adequate trump support and an ace somewhere in the hand, but it is more descriptive to bid three diamonds, intending to support spades on the next round. Over two hearts make the negative response of two no-trumps in the first place. Yes, if the opening had been two diamonds you would raise to three diamonds, but you and partner appear to have an awful lot of diamonds and not much outside!

Hand (b) contains 8 points. To an opening two no-trumps you could try a Stayman or a Baron three club bid, looking for a safer major suit game, but you should be prepared to settle for three no-trumps if partner doesn't come up with a fit for you. An opening of two hearts or two spades could be raised direct to game, a response that shows a good trump fit and no first-round control. However, in classical Acol, the responder is supposed to have two kings for that bid, so you may prefer to give a negative response first. If the opening bid were two diamonds, caution is needed. Give a negative response of two no-trumps in the first instance and see what develops. You mustn't jump to four diamonds because for one thing your trump support isn't good, and a bid of three diamonds would, of course, promise an ace or void. If partner opens two clubs you've got the necessary 8 points for a positive response, and you could simply bid two no-trumps. If you think you have a 'bad' 8, and it is best to start with a negative Two Diamonds, you may well be right.

Hand (c) contains a similar point. In response to two clubs it looks like an obvious positive bid and therefore a jump to three diamonds – because two diamonds would be the conventional negative. This is just what we would have told you to do until fairly recently. However, suppose over your three diamonds partner comes back with three spades. Do you show your heart suit and by-pass the possible best contract of three no-trumps, or do you sign off with three no-trumps yourself and find you have missed a heart or no-trump slam?

Our advice to you is, do not use up bidding space unless you know where you plan to end up. Just bid two diamonds – which partner will understand (and tell the opposition if they ask) to be 'negative until proved positive'. Now when he rebids two spades you can bid three diamonds, showing a genuine diamond suit, and forward-going values. If partner now has a four-card heart suit, he has room to show it. In any event, the partnership will have given itself every opportunity to arrive in the right game or slam.

Remember, this 'negative until proved positive' sequence only applies over openings of two clubs, because the bid has not as yet conveyed any genuine information other than that opener has a powerhouse. Over openings of two no-trumps there is, of course, no negative but pass, and over strong twos, as opener has named his suit, there is no need to conserve space and a two no-trump negative response is exactly that – partner, I have nothing better to say.

Now here are three hands that you might be lucky enough to pick up sometime, and it would be a great pity not to know how to describe them accurately:

(a) ♠ K Q J 10 9   (b) ♠ A K Q 2   (c) ♠ K Q J 10 6 5
    ♡ K Q J 10 9   ♡ A K   ♡ A K 7
    ◇ K Q   ◇ K Q J   ◇ 6
    ♣ K   ♣ K Q J 4   ♣ A K Q

Hand (a) is our old friend, the one that people who insist on counting points will always get wrong. You have 20 points, but you can't count full value for the bare king of clubs, so it's clearly worth less. With a singleton, you can't contemplate opening two no-trumps. Equally clearly the hand isn't worth a two club opening. If we prefer weak two bids, we would have to open one spade in any event.

Hand (b) is quite definitely a two club opening, but watch your rebid! Over a negative two diamonds just bid three no-trumps, bidding the game most likely to make. Be careful if you get a positive response of, say, two hearts, not to jump to three no-trumps. This would simply promise 25+ points, and responder might pass. You must make a slam try at once, and a direct 'Blackwood' four no-trumps is the right bid. This will make sure you don't miss bidding a grand slam if responder happens to hold both missing aces.

Hand (c) is another special case. If after your obvious opening two clubs, partner responds two diamonds, don't abandon all hopes of a slam. Remember, his hand may not be really a negative. Rebid three spades, to show your excellent suit and asking partner to name an ace, if he happens to have one. If he doesn't he will just rebid three no-trumps, no matter what he holds in the way of a diamond suit, because for him to bid four diamonds over your three spades would promise the diamond ace. If by any glorious chance he happened to have both the missing aces, you will be well on the way to a grand slam.

Baron Three Clubs Convention

There are other ways than 'Stayman' of trying to locate a fit when partner has opened two no-trumps, or rebid two no-trumps in the sequence 2♣ – 2◇ – 2NT. You may prefer to adopt the 'Baron three clubs' convention instead. Whereas Stayman can locate a major suit fit, Baron is designed to locate any 4-4 fit (or better) that exists. When partner has opened two no-trumps (20–22 points) or shown 23–24 points by opening two clubs and rebidding two no-trumps, three clubs from responder now asks for opener's four-card suit or suits in ascending order.

One of the great values of this convention is that it facilitates the otherwise difficult-to-reach minor suit slams. You must be careful that you are on the same wavelength as your partner before you embark on a 'Baron' sequence – nothing but disaster is likely to result if one of you is playing 'Baron' and the other 'Stayman'! Here, then, are the responses opener will make if responder bids a 'Baron' three clubs:

3NT   a four (or five)-card club suit and no other four-card suit

3◇   a four (or five)-card diamond suit, and possibly any other four-card suit

3♡   a four (or five)-card heart suit, possibly a four-card black suit, but not a four-card diamond suit

3♠   a four (or five)-card spade suit, possibly a four-card club suit, but no four-card red suit.

Here's just one opener's hand, with two hands responder might hold, to give you an idea of how the convention works:

Opener	Responder	
♠ A K 8 7	(a) ♠ Q J 5 2	(b) ♠ Q 9 3
♡ A Q 7	♡ J 10 6 4	♡ K J 9 6
◇ A J 8 6	◇ 7	◇ K Q 9 7
♣ K 9	♣ 8 7 4 2	♣ 8 4

On opener's hand facing the first responder's hand the bidding would go:

    2NT   3♣
    3◇   3♡
    3♠   4♠

On opener's hand opposite the second responder's hand the bidding might begin:

    2NT   3♣
    3◇   3♡
    3♠   4◇

15
Some Slam Bidding Conventions

The Blackwood Convention

This is one of the first conventions that newcomers to the game are taught. Many students are given the impression that all slams are bid by way of this convention, and that it is a crime to bid any slam without proceeding by way of four no-trumps and then five no-trumps! This, is far from true, and you will find that there are many potential slam hands on which 'Blackwood' is useless.

A 'Blackwood' enquiry, first for aces and then for kings (but only if the reply to four no-trumps shows that all four aces are held) is useful when the precise number of controls held needs to be known. The convention is, therefore, usually used for bidding slams in suits, but beware the dangers of 'Blackwood in the minors'. If, for example, you're heading for a club slam and need partner to hold two aces, remember that a one-ace response to four no-trumps is five diamonds, which drives you to six clubs whether you like it or not!

Another situation where Blackwood will not provide the answer is when there are voids around. In that situation you should try and gather the information you need by means of cue bidding.

The Gerber Convention

The Gerber Convention is not a substitute for 'Blackwood'. You and your partner can agree to play both, but be sure to choose the right occasion before you use either. Gerber is reserved for use when partner has opened one no-trump or two no-trumps and you, knowing the strength of his hand in terms of points, want to know how many aces and kings it includes.

Responding to a no-trump opening bid only, an immediate bid of four clubs has nothing whatever to do with the club suit but is simply a question that demands an answer! Opener's rebids to show aces are:

4◇	0 or 4 aces
4♡	1 ace
4♠	2 aces
4NT	3 aces

If the partnership now wishes to check on the number of kings held, the bid of five clubs asks the question and the same replies at the five level give the answer. After the original four club bid and response, any bid other than five clubs is a sign-off and must be passed by the no-trump opener.

It follows, therefore, that if responder suspects a contract of five clubs is the right resting-place the Gerber Convention cannot be employed!

There comes a time in the career of most players when a friend triumphantly explains the existence of 'Gerber' and points out that it keeps the bidding lower than a 'Blackwood' four no-trumps and must, therefore, be much better when the slam is not there after all. The answer to this is that 'Gerber' is an excellent convention used in its proper place, which is after a no-trump opening bid.

If the wrong ace-answer to a 'Blackwood' enquiry will take you above the safe sign-off level, then you have bid badly or too quickly in the early stages of the auction, or should have used cue-bidding instead of a general ace-asking bid anyway.

(a) ♠ K 8 2	(b) ♠ A J 10 7 6 5	(c) ♠ K Q J 8 7
♡ Q 6 3	♡ 4	♡ —
◇ A J 9 4	◇ K Q 8 7 4	◇ 6 5 3
♣ Q 5 2	♣ 2	♣ A K 7 6 5

Hand (a) is easy to bid provided you and your partner are using your quantitative raises in no-trumps correctly. To an opening bid of two no-trumps simply bid four no-trumps, knowing that with a good 21+ your partner will bid the slam. If he makes the awful error of treating your four no-trumps as 'Blackwood' and responds by showing you the number of aces he has, it won't help you to decide on whether or not to bid the slam. Remember that the more points he has tied up in aces, the more likely he is, with only 20 points, to lose a couple of tricks to the missing kings and queens!

Hand (b) doesn't contain nearly as many points, but a slam is equally likely if opener has the right cards. Now it really is only aces you're interested in, so bid a 'Gerber' four clubs over the two no-trump opening. In spite of your splendid distribution, you don't want to find yourself in an unmakeable six spades missing two aces. Granted, it's very difficult to construct a hand for opener that doesn't have two aces, but it can be done. The alternative approach on this type of hand is to bid both your suits. You would respond three spades, and hope to introduce your diamonds on the next round. Both methods are likely to lead to a sensible contract.

Holding hand (c) when your partner opens two no-trumps, you will bid three spades and, if he raises to four spades you can cue bid five clubs, showing the ace of clubs, hoping that he will then show the vital ace of diamonds. If you make any other slam try you will only find out how many points or how many aces the two no-trump opening holds, and it will be too late when dummy goes down and you see that it contains the useless ace of hearts and not the ace of diamonds.

There's one other point to be made for the sake of those who still hanker after using 'Gerber' because 'Blackwood' may drive you too high. Firstly, if you can't safely play at the five-level, you shouldn't be looking for a slam, so you ought to be able to afford to be driven that far. Secondly, you are not, using 'Blackwood', necessarily forced to go to a six contract once you've bid four no-trumps. Take, for instance, a sequence such as this:

North	South
1♡	3♣
4♣	4♡
4NT	5◇
?	

When North decides to go slamming after South's force, and bids four no-trumps, South turns up with one ace less than North had hoped for, so he simply signs off in five of the agreed suit, hearts.

There is also another sequence that will leave you quietly playing in five no-trumps.

North	South
1♡	3◇
4◇	4NT
5◇	5♠
5NT	

In the auction above, South's four no-trumps enquiry has discovered one ace too few in the North hand. South now has three options – he could pass five diamonds, an agreed suit or, if holding heart support, could convert to five hearts. He is, however, playing match-point pairs, so prefers to play in the higher-scoring no-trump contract. He can't bid five no-trumps himself as this would be a request to North to show kings, but he can bid five of any unbid suit (in this case spades) which instructs North to convert to five no-trumps, which South will pass.

Cue Bidding

The point at which an exploratory bid gives way to a cue bid is when a suit has been agreed – either directly or by inference – the partnership is committed to game, and it's obvious that the time has come to make a slam try.

A cue bid is one that shows a control in a side suit. It is usually a first round control, either the ace or a void, but in certain situations it may be a second round control, the king or a singleton.

It suggests to partner that a slam try may be in the offing, and that the cue-bidder would like to exchange information about other controls held by the partnership. It follows, therefore, that the majority of cue bids are made when the partnership has agreed a suit and it is only the final level of the contract, game or slam, which has to be settled. Let's look at a few examples which will help to explain.

♠ A 2
♡ K J 9 8
♢ K 9 7 6
♣ K 8 6

As dealer you open this hand with one no-trump, and partner responds three hearts, promising a powerful hand with a heart suit. Before you raise to four hearts and proudly put down what is certainly a lovely dummy for a partner who wants to play in at least a game in hearts, think how much your hand has improved in the light of responder's bid. So make a bid of three spades. This gives very precise information, showing trump (hearts) agreement, first round control of spades (which must be an ace as you wouldn't have opened one no-trump with a void in spades), and a maximum for your opening bid. If not interested, partner can just convert to four hearts, but if the knowledge gained makes him enthusiastic about a slam, partner can make a return cue bid of his own.

When making a cue bid, you should normally do so in the lowest, or cheapest suit available.

♠ A 2
♥ K 10 9 8
♦ A 9 7 6
♣ K 8 6

In the previous example the ace of spades was your only first round control. But had you held a second ace, as in the above version of the hand, your ace of spades would still have been your cheapest control as you could show it at the three-level, whilst it would be necessary to go on to the four-level to show the ace of diamonds. After your three spade bid, if your partner cue-bids four clubs, you can show your diamond control with four diamonds.

Change the hand again, making it:

♠ K 2
♥ K 10 9 8
♦ A 9 7 6
♣ A 8 6

Now your cheapest first round control is the ace of clubs, and if you bid four clubs, you will be denying the ace of spades as you missed out the cheaper three spade bid. Suppose partner made a return cue bid of four diamonds – what would you make of that? Well, as you've got the ace of diamonds, it must be showing either the king of diamonds or a void or singleton in that suit. You can now afford to show your second round spade control by bidding four spades.

Cue bids can be made by either member of the partnership, so let's look at another example.

♠ Q 5
♥ K J 10 8 4
♦ A 10 9 5
♣ A 7

You hear your partner open one club, and respond one heart. Partner now rebids three hearts and, with every intention of going at least to game, you realise you hold a much better hand than you need for your bidding thus far, in addition to which partner's rebid has strengthened your hand still further. You might think at this point that you should stick to the rule we have given you of cue-bidding your lowest control, which would be rebidding four clubs.

But it's possible to be a bit clever here. If you bid four clubs, partner's cheapest control might be a diamond void which is not what you want to hear. Bid four diamonds – partner will know quickly enough if this doubles up with a void in his hand, but it leaves him free to make a return cue bid of four spades if he has the ace of spades, and that's just what you are looking for. You can cue-bid your ace of clubs and leave the next move to your partner.

You can see from this that it's possible to pinpoint whether or not a specific control is held and, thereafter, to bid or stay out of a slam without ever having to go through the motions of 'Blackwood'. If you use Blackwood, and get a five diamond one ace reply you will for ever be in the dark as to which ace partner holds, when a cue-bidding sequence would have told you.

Look at these two hands and work out how easy it is to bid them using cue bids:

Opener		*Responder*
♠ K Q J 10 8		♠ A 7 6
♡ A 9 8 4		♡ K Q J 5 3
◇ A Q		◇ K J 4
♣ 7 6		♣ 4 2

You open one spade, and your partner responds two hearts. You show your strong hand by a jump to four hearts. Don't by the way, make the mistake of thinking this is a 'stop' bid – far from it – it is simply that you don't want to risk the bidding stopping before game is reached. This should jerk your partner into action as he, too, has a pretty good hand. If you held his cards would you now bid a Blackwood four no-trumps, as a slam certainly seems a possibility? If you did you would find that partner held two aces, so you might well decide to go on to six hearts. As you can see, if the enemy find the club lead, you are down at once.

The responder should look far enough ahead to see that the little doubleton club, with the lead coming through any club honour you may hold, spells danger. He tries to find out, by making a cue bid of four spades, over four hearts, whether you have a club control. You are equally interested in a slam, and take up the invitation by bidding your own lowest control with a return cue bid of five diamonds. Now partner knows that neither player controls clubs, as you would have shown either the ace of clubs or a club void before showing the diamond control, so he reluctantly signs off in five hearts. He may well make all thirteen tricks on any other lead than a club but, as things are, to bid a slam would be a gamble.

Cue Bidding After the Suit Has Been Agreed by Inference

As any raise of partner's suit, even to game, is never a forcing bid, only a highly-invitational one, it is sometimes possible – and advisable – to make a jump cue-bid, the meaning of which is that you want to play at least as high as game, and still have mild slam ambitions. Look at responder's problem on the deal below:

Opener		Responder
♠ A K J 8 4		♠ Q 10 2
♡ 7 3	N	♡ A K Q J 8
◇ K J 4	W E	◇ A 8
♣ J 6 2	S	♣ 10 4 3

The bidding has gone 1♠ – 2♡ – 2♠. If responder now bids four spades, opener will pass and a slam may have been missed. If responder bids four no-trumps, the contract will end up at five spades, and the defenders can take the first three tricks in clubs. The solution is for responder's second bid to be four diamonds. This advance cue bid agrees spades as trumps, and promises the ace or a void in diamonds, and denies a first round control in clubs. Opener has no difficulty in signing off with four spades.

16
Quantitative Bidding

As we are sure you have already appreciated, the Acol system of bidding is based on the use of quantitative bids wherever possible. The first quantitative bids you learned were the Acol limit bids, both in suits and no-trumps, but the ones that often finished beyond a game were the direct raises in no-trumps, where no suit has been mentioned by either partner, the scale for which is set out below. So before you carry on with this topic, make sure you understand completely the principles behind the direct no-trump raises.

1NT opened:		2NT opened:	
Holding:		Holding:	
11–12 points	bid 2NT	4–10 points	bid 3NT
13–18 points	bid 3NT	11–12 points	bid 4NT
19–20 points	bid 4NT	13–14 points	bid 6NT
21–22 points	bid 6NT	15–16 points	bid 5NT
23–24 points	bid 5NT	17+ points	bid 7NT
25+ points	bid 7NT		

Important:

The bids of three no-trumps, six no-trumps and seven no-trumps in both tables are limit bids. Four no-trumps is invitational and five no-trumps is unconditionally forcing on opener to choose between the small and grand slams. It must *not* be passed!

The bids you have learned thus far, although they are quantitative, are generally referred to as limit bids, but the real quantitative bids are used to invite partner to bid beyond game level, to a slam if possible, as long as he holds precisely the right cards. They are always invitational, and are used when you haven't got a more expressive bid. They frequently occur when you are worried about a control in a particular suit. This may be an unbid suit, or one bid by the opposition, or, as you will see from this first example, simply because you need partner to hold a bit more strength than he has already shown.

Let's look at a hand where you are East, and your partner is bidding strongly. If you don't listen very carefully to the bidding, you won't be able to appreciate what a goldmine your hand has become:

♠ Q 8 4	**West**	**East**
♡ Q J 10 6	2♣	2◇
◇ 7 5 4 2	2♠	2NT
♣ 7 6	3♡	?

When West makes that bid of three hearts, East should really sit up and take notice! His partner has announced a rock-crushing hand with five quick tricks and quite certainly not less than five spades and four hearts. East's queen of spades now becomes a key card, and his heart holding almost certainly guarantees no trump losers for a partner playing in hearts. Partner can't possibly have more than two minor suit losers, and may very well have only one. So don't make the sign-off bid of four hearts – try a quantitative bid of five hearts saying that, in spite of your initial negative all your values are in the right place.

Now let's look at a couple of different hands which would fit West's bidding:

(a) ♠ A K J 10 9	(b) ♠ A J 10 9 8
♡ A K 9 7	♡ A K 9 7
◇ A 9	◇ K 7
♣ A 4	♣ A K

With hand (a) West will certainly raise five hearts to six hearts. He will reckon that your invitational raise must be based on a useful card and a good heart fit. On (b) he may decide to pass. He knows the ace of diamonds is missing, and there may be a spade loser.

Now we'll have another example that is along the same lines – East recognising the value of very minimal assets.

		West	East
♠	Q 8 4	2♣	2◇
♡	8 4	2♠	3♠
◇	8 6 4 3 2	4♣	4♠
♣	K 7 2	5◇	?

In spite of the fact that East has signed off, West is making a slam try – his five diamond bid can be nothing else – and he's doing that although he can't know that his partner holds both the queen of the agreed trump suit and the king in his second suit. East mustn't just bid five spades over five diamonds but must jump to six spades. Go back to West's bidding and you'll find it difficult to construct a hand on which he won't be able to bid the grand slam. He must be holding a massive heart/club two-suiter, quite possibly with a void in hearts.

Control in an Unbid Suit

Now let's look at a different situation – one where a quantitative bid can be used to check up on the need for a control in a specific suit. This usually happens when a partnership has bid three suits and the slam depends on whether one or two tricks may be lost in the fourth suit..

♠	5			♠	A J 10 9 4
♡	A J 10 8 6 3	**N**		♡	K Q 7
◇	K Q	**W E**		◇	6 2
♣	A K 9 4	**S**		♣	Q J 10

West	East
1♡	1♠
3♣	5♡
6♡	

When West rebids three clubs, showing a strong hand with a good heart suit, East immediately has visions of a slam. A Blackwood bid of four no-trumps will only tell him that West holds two aces, almost certainly the ace of hearts and ace of clubs. East knows that the opposition, for whom the diamond weakness has been pinpointed, could start off by cashing the ◇ A- K. He wants to know is whether West has a diamond control, and his bid of five hearts asks this specific question. Had West held the king of spades instead of the king of diamonds, he would have passed the bid of five hearts.

Control of the Opponents' Suit

We have just seen how the use of a quantitative bid saw us through the situation where control of the fourth, unbid, suit was needed. Now, let's look at a couple of deals where the slam rests on whether the partnership has more than one loser in the suit bid by the opposition. What would you do if you held the following hand in fourth position, when dealer had been inconsiderate enough to open with a bid of Three Hearts, over which your partner bid three spades? If partner holds hand (a) there's a certain slam on, and if he holds hand (b) there's equally certainly no slam!

	(a)	(b)
♠ K J 4	♠ A Q 10 9 8 6 5	♠ A Q 10 9 8 6 5
♡ 6 4	♡ 3	♡ 7 3
◇ A 4	◇ K 6 5	◇ K Q
♣ A K Q J 10 2	♣ 5 4	♣ 5 4

His bid has promised a good six or seven-card suit, with a little outside, which, as you have the ♠ K-J, is almost certainly in diamonds. It's obvious that the hand will play splendidly in spades because your club suit will absorb all partner's losers. But if the defence can take the first two tricks in hearts, partner will not thank you for bidding a slam. The way to find out if partner can control the heart suit is to bid a direct five spades. This specifically draws partner's attention to the enemy suit – hearts. It requires complete trust and confidence in your bidding, but holding hand (a) he should bid the cold six spades, and on hand (b) he must equally trustingly pass.

The deal laid out below is another illustration of just how valuable these control-asking bids can be:

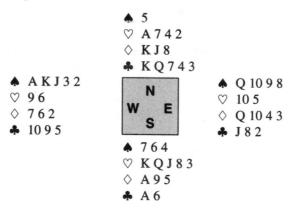

The bidding went as follows:

West	North	East	South
–	1♣	Pass	1♡
1♠	3♡	3♠	4◇
Pass	4♡	Pass	5♡
Pass	6♡	All Pass	

When West bid spades, East showed support in case West wanted to sacrifice. South's bid of four diamonds was, a cue bid. North, with no other first round control to show, retreated to four hearts. Now South, holding the ace of clubs, wanted to bid the slam, but didn't dare to do so in case there were two spade losers in the North hand. He, therefore, used a quantitative bid of five hearts, asking North specifically about his spade holding. With second-round control of the suit, North was able to bid the slam.

Notice that West could have made life much more difficult by bidding four spades over four diamonds. North-South might still have bid the slam, but not with such certainty.

Summary

1   **A quantitative bid may be made in no-trumps, where it checks on the point count held, or in a suit, where it asks for controls.**

2   **It is a bid which carries the partnership beyond game level.**

3   **It denies the ability to make a more expressive bid.**

When a Bid of Four No-Trumps is Quantitative or Ace-Asking

Before we finish this chapter let's just have a look at the tricky question of distinguishing between a quantitative bid of four no-trumps or when it is one of the slam convention varieties. Misinterpretation is easy, and hard and fast rules are difficult to lay down. You are very much in the realm of partnership understanding and common sense, but here are some general rules for guidance.

A bid of four no-trumps when neither member of the partnership has bid a suit genuinely is always quantitative.

1	1NT	4NT		2	2NT	5NT
3	1NT	2♣		4	2♣	2◇
	2◇	4NT			3NT	4NT
5	1♡	1♠		6	1♠	3NT
	3♠	4NT			4NT	
7	1♡	2♠				
	3NT	4NT				

In each of the first four sequences the final bids are clearly quantitative, as the suit bids used are all conventional. Nos 1, 3, and 4 can be passed if opener has already said his all and No 2 demands that opener should bid the small slam on a minimum hand and the grand slam on a maximum hand.

No 5 is obviously not quantitative as spades have been agreed as trumps and controls, that is aces, are what are required for suit slams. No 6 is a tricky one, as opener may well want to know the number of controls held, not the point count of the three no-trump bid, and it is as well to agree the meaning of this sequence between yourself and your partner. One thing is clear – it must be a slam try. Much the same applies in sequence No 7, as both partnerships are showing strong hands –controls are going to be more important than points.

Here is a further sequence for you to look at:

> 1NT   2♣
> 2♡   4NT

This is generally considered to be quantitative, not Blackwood. The reason is that if at this point you want to ask for aces, then you can use a bid of four clubs, the Gerber Convention.

Here's a last word of advice about quantitative bids of four no-trumps. If you are the partner of the player who makes the call, and you aren't absolutely sure as to whether he means it as quantitative or conventional, treat it as conventional and give him the ace-answer. This will give him the chance to bid the slam he is angling for, even if perhaps it turns out to have been the wrong thing to do. He'll forgive you much more readily than if you pass his four no-trumps when he was merely trying to find out whether to finish in six spades or go to seven spades!

17
Take-out Doubles

A double made by a player who has not previously had a chance to bid, and whose partner has not bid in a low-level situation is, with one exception, for take-out, the exception being when the opening bid had been one no-trump. A double of one no-trump is always intended primarily for penalties and won't be taken out except for some very good reason. If your partner has already bid, other than to pass, then your double is always intended as a penalty one.

With regard to this last point, you may meet players whose doubles at a low level are not necessarily for take-out. To make this clear, take this sequence.

West	North	East	South
–	1♡	2◇	Double

When you, sitting South, double East's two diamonds, you intend it for penalties.

In recent years it has become fashionable to treat this type of double in a different way.

Negative Double

The American Alvin Roth is widely recognised as one of the most original bidding theorists in the history of bridge. His many contributions to the language of bidding include the unusual no-trump, the forcing no-trump response and even an entire system, Roth-Stone.

Perhaps his greatest discovery is the *negative double*, a convention that is probably used more than a million times a day in bridge tournaments all over the world. Some years later, the Russians were busy with their space satellite programme and the name Sputnik became linked to the idea.

Before the advent of the negative double if an opponent overcalled the opening bid a double was for penalties. Roth realised that it would be more useful to use the bid as a take-out device. Here is an example of the convention in action:

♠ 9 6 3	West	North	East	South
♡ K J 7 4	1♣	1♠	?	
◇ A 8 6 3				
♣ 7 5				

You have excellent support for the unbid suits but can hardly bid either of them. By using a negative double you promise at least the values to respond at the one level. If the overcall is in a major the double promises at least four cards in the other one.

Its important to understand that if you wanted to double the overcall for penalties you have to pass! Your partner is then expected to reopen the bidding with a double. Here is an illustration:

♠ A K 10 9 4	West	North	East	South
♡ 4	1♠	2♡	Pass	Pass
◇ A J 6 4	?			
♣ 8 5 3				

Rather than rebid his spades West should double, hoping to find East with a hand like:

♠ 7 3
♡ K J 9 7 5
◇ Q 10 7
♣ A 10 4

Even if you have excellent support for partner's suit it may be correct to start with a negative double.

♠ 10 7	West	North	East	South
♡ K Q 7 4	1♣	1♠	?	
◇ 8 7				
♣ K J 9 5 4				

Of course you could support clubs at once but then you would risk losing the heart suit. By starting with a double you inform partner that you have at least four hearts. If he bids two diamonds you will reveal the nature of your hand by bidding three clubs.

Our advice is to forget about using a double in this way until you are a great deal more experienced, though do find out from your opponents what their doubles in this position really mean. Meanwhile we prefer our doubles, especially if our opponents intervene rashly at the two level, to be to punish them for getting into our auction!

Requirements for a Take-Out Double

When you make a take-out double, especially if your partner has already passed, you will be expected to hold opening bid values, and a tolerance for each of the three unbid suits, unless you have a much better than average point count, i.e. 16+. Tolerance is a holding of at least three cards in the suit. This is because if the double passes round to your partner, he may be forced to bid on next to nothing in the way of points, except when he can convert your take-out double into a penalty double. To do this he must be holding very good trumps and a probable trick in one of your suits.

Paradoxically, particularly if yours is the vulnerable side and partner has an even stronger hand, it might well be that he should bid two no-trumps to suggest game is on for your side. The point is that defeating a non-vulnerable opener by one or two tricks will not be sufficient recompense for a making game.

To double a major suit opened generally shows an interest in finding a fit with partner in the unbid major, and almost invariably guarantees a four-card holding. Avoid overcalling in a four-card suit, even at the one level. If you have the values to be bidding at all, you will almost invariably be better to double for take-out or overcall one no-trump. Of course, you must not even consider overcalling in a four-card suit at the two level!

Look at the following hands. In each case the opening was one spade.

(a) ♠ 7 2	(b) ♠ 7 2	(c) ♠ A 2
♡ A Q 10	♡ A 10 9	♡ K 4 3
◇ K J 9 2	◇ A K 9 8 7	◇ A Q 9 4
♣ A Q 9 2	♣ Q 8 7	♣ K J 6 2

With hand (a) you will make your take-out double, even though you do not have four hearts. With such good outside values even if partner ends up in a 4-3 trump fit, it should have reasonable chances of making. Holding hand (b), just forget about doubling. Your hearts are not very good and the overall quality of the hand is less good. The only positive action you can consider is two diamonds. We would prefer a stronger suit or even better a sixth diamond, and we would recommend a pass at this point. Hand (c) is much better described by an overcall of one no-trump. We agree that your spade holding is not ideal, but to double without the hearts on such a flat hand is also risky..

Responding to a Take-Out Double

If your partner makes a take-out double, and opener's partner does not bid, the worse your hand the more essential it is that you bid – something! Of course, if opener's partner has bid, then you will bid if you feel you have something worthwhile to say. Remember that your partner wants to compete. Stretch everything to bid if the response has simply been to raise the suit opened. Let's look at a few examples. The opening bid has been 1♡, your partner has doubled, and third player has passed.

(a) ♠ J 9 4 2	(b) ♠ J 9 2	(c) ♠ J 9 2
♡ 7 6 4 2	♡ 7 6 4 2	♡ 7 6 4 2
◇ Q 9 3	◇ J 5 3 2	◇ 8
♣ J 4	♣ 10 6	♣ A 9 5 4 2

Holding hand (a) you have an obvious bid of one spade, exactly the suit partner is hoping you will bid. With hand (b) you must resist the temptation to pass, and respond two diamonds. On hand (c) you will, of course, bid a natural two clubs. Note that every time you held length in hearts. This is more than likely whenever partner doubles for take-out, because if opener's partner had length in his suit, he needs little in the way of points to give an interference raise just to make life difficult for you.

Here are three more hands for you to study.

(d) ♠ K Q 8 4 3	(e) ♠ Q 4	(f) ♠ A 4
♡ 7 6 4 2	♡ A J 9	♡ Q J 9 8 7
◇ K 4	◇ Q 7 6 5	◇ 8 5 4
♣ Q 2	♣ 10 9 8 6	♣ 7 5 3

On hand (d) you are delighted to bid, but be careful not to say just one spade, or partner will picture you with a hand like (a) and will drop the bidding when game may well be on. Bid a cheerful three spades. Hand (e) is a sound call of one no-trump, showing your heart stops. Partner will know you have no interest in spades, the unbid major, and may well be able to bid the no-trump game. Hand (f) is the one for passing, telling partner you are confident of beating opener's one heart and that you are sure taking the certain penalty will be more profitable than any part-score your side might make.

Responding to Opener After a Take-Out Double

The doubler wants to contest the hand and to bring his partner into the auction. If you really can find nothing to say, then you must pass, or you might encourage your partner to bid too high and incur a large penalty. Let's consider the following hands that you might hold when your partner has bid one heart and your right-hand opponent doubles.

(a) ♠ 7 2	(b) ♠ A J 9 8	(c) ♠ A 10 2
♡ A 5 4 2	♡ 8 3	♡ 8 3
◇ 10 4 3	◇ 8 5 2	◇ K 10 3 2
♣ 9 7 4 2	♣ K 4 3 2	♣ J 10 9 3

With hand (a) raise to two hearts, and if the ten of diamonds were to become the king of diamonds you would bid three hearts, each time bidding one level higher than you would if the other side had not intervened. Hand (b) is just a change of suit to one spade, the bid you would have made if there had been no intervention. Your bid is forcing for one round. On hand (c) bid one no-trump, again your natural call over an opening one heart.

(d) ♠ Q J 10 8 7 2	(e) ♠ A K 2	(f) ♠ 9 4
♡ 4	♡ 4 2	♡ A Q 9 3
◇ Q 7 2	◇ Q 9 7 3	◇ K 5 4 3
♣ 5 4 3	♣ Q 8 6 3	♣ K 8 2

Hand (d) is a jump response of two spades, showing a long weak suit which must be trumps, absolutely no fit with partner's suit, and no defensive values. Your bid is, of course, most certainly non-forcing. With (e) just redouble to show values, no fit with partner and the balance of points for your side. You are looking for a nice penalty. Don't make the mistake of redoubling with hand (f). You have far too good a fit with partner to want to defend. Bid a conventional two no-trumps to show a sound raise to three hearts and let partner judge whether to convert to three hearts or four hearts. Remember that two no-trumps is conventional because with a good hand that was interested in trying to take a penalty, you would start with a redouble.

Double and Bid Afterwards

Shown below are three hands on which the best move is a take-out double to begin with. But you do not intend, almost certainly, to accept your partner's choice of response. Here, opener's bid was one heart.

(a)	♠ A K J 9 6	(b)	♠ A K Q J 10 7	(c)	♠ A K 2
	♡ 4		♡ A 6		♡ A J 10
	◇ A Q 9 4 3		◇ K 9 8		◇ A J 9 6
	♣ K 9		♣ J 4		♣ Q 6 5

The first hand is an excellent two-suiter. When you double you are almost certain to hear a response of two clubs. Now bid two spades, showing no interest in partner's clubs and effectively bidding your diamond suit as well. How should partner know this? Well, you did ask his opinion, and disregarded it, didn't you, and had you had a single-suited hand too strong for an immediate jump overcall, you would have jumped to three spades over his bid, as with hand (b). Hand (c) is far too strong to overcall one no-trump at once, so just double and over partner's reply, no matter what his choice of suit, rebid in no-trumps.

Cue-Bid Overcall

This is an immediate intervening bid in the suit opened on your right. Suppose yourself to hold any of the following hands in second seat and hear an opening bid of one spade.

(a)	♠ 7	(b)	♠ —	(c)	♠ K 4
	♡ A K Q 9 8 6 2		♡ A K Q J 3		♡ A K
	◇ K Q 3		◇ A J 9 7		◇ A Q J 8 5 4
	♣ A 7		♣ K Q 6 2		♣ A 9 8

Beginners know that you never offer as trumps a suit already bid in a natural sense by the other side, so this bid can be clearly understood by your partner to say that you have an absolute rockcrusher of a hand on which you were all poised to open with a two-level bid when your right-hand opponent unexpectedly opened in front of you. The danger of making a simple make-out double on this type of hand is that your partner, with most of his assets in the opponent's suit, will pass for penalties. You will almost certainly extract a penalty, but one which is unlikely to compensate for a missed game or slam your way.

Generally speaking, this cue bid overcall won't contain more than one loser in the suit you are cue bidding. As the cue bid is unconditionally forcing to game, your partner must recognise that he won't need much in his hand to go on to a slam once you and he have found a fit. Above all, he won't expect you to have two losers in the suit originally opened. An example of this comes from a recent match, when the opponent overcalled the opening one heart with two hearts on this hand.

♠ A K Q J 10 2
♡ 7 4
♢ —
♣ A K J 10 5

His partner, with the ace of diamonds and a six-card club suit to the queen, 'knew' the overcaller couldn't have more than one heart loser, and when his four clubs was raised to five clubs, he happily bid six clubs. Unfortunately the opponents cashed the ♡ A-K. At the other table the overcaller merely doubled, and they finished in five clubs, which couldn't be defeated.

Before we go on to the next item we should, perhaps, point out that some partnerships play the cue bid overcall as forcing to suit agreement only, meaning that once a fit has been found the bidding may be dropped by either partner, even if game has not been reached. We, however, like to feel we have one bid with which we can be quite certain that we can force partner to keep the bidding open until a game contract has been reached. This leaves us more bidding space to explore for the best fit, and also means that it's never necessary to jump to game to make sure of getting there, which may well mean missing an easy slam.

Unusual No-Trump Overcall

Here is another very useful overcall, which belongs in the family of 'asking' intervening bids. It is most often used for what we call an 'advance sacrifice', and most commonly by a non-vulnerable partnership against vulnerable opponents.

It works like this. A major suit is opened by a player on the right of an opponent who has great length in both minor suits and next to no defence against a game contract in either major, so he makes an overcall of two no-trumps. This is certainly unusual, isn't it?

So systems have attached a special meaning to the bid, which has nothing to do with 'no-trumps'!

The two no-trump bid doesn't have to be in the immediate overcalling position. Say the bidding has gone:

West	North	East	South
–	–	–	1♠
Pass	2♡	2NT	

Two no-trumps would be very unusual as a natural bid in this situation, so it is the unusual no-trump, asking for West's preference between the minors.

The bidder of the unusual no-trump is telling his partner that he has at least 5–5 in the two minor suits, preferably 6–5 or even 6–6, and asks his partner to continue the obstruction of the opposition bidding by showing his better minor suit. If opener's partner passes over the two no-trump overcall, then fourth player must bid his better minor, even if it's the choice between as little as a doubleton and a singleton. There may, of course, be very rare occasions when the player required to respond to the two no-trump bid may have such good major suit holdings that he is prepared to play in two no-trumps, perhaps doubled, knowing that the hand facing him will have nothing but length in the minors.

It is very satisfactory to play in five clubs doubled, even going two down, when the enemy could make ten tricks in hearts or spades! – and even more delightful when they could have made twelve tricks in their major suit.

Of course, there is a downside to this type of bid, it gives away a lot of information about your distribution, and that will be helpful to the declarer if your side ends up defending.

18
Doubling Opening Bids of One No-Trump

In the first chapter of this book we strongly advised you to use a one no-trump opening bid of 12–14 points, whatever the vulnerability. We're well aware that occasionally it comes unstuck, and the opposition can double us for penalties, and get a far better score than by bidding on themselves, because they had no game on their way. When this happens, you must shrug your shoulders philosophically, and remind yourself and partner of the many times when, by opening weak, you have stopped your opponents from getting into the auction at all, or prevented them from bidding up to their rightful game or part-score.

Now we'll move you into the seat on the left of the opponent who has dealt and opened with a weak no-trump.

Just because you hold a hand on which you would yourself have opened the bidding – perhaps a balanced 12–14 points or 12 or 13 points with a five-card suit, you don't necessarily have the right cards to bid over the opening no-trump. You may just have to pass and hope declarer will go down anyway – which he may well not do!

There are several conventions to choose from when you are ready to compete against an opening bid of one no-trump artificially by trying to find a fit with your partner's hand, and to make a contract your way, or possibly drive the no-trump bidder and his partner too high. When you make one of these conventional asking bids, you tell your partner two things. Firstly, you haven't got the right cards with which to double the opening bid for penalties and exact a big enough penalty and secondly, that you need his opinion as to the right place to play the contract your way.

Requirements for Making a Penalty Double

A double of an opening one no-trump bid is always intended primarily for penalties, and should be left in by partner in the great majority of cases.

Let's look at what you do mean when you double. You promise a hand holding 16 high-card points or possibly a good 15 points with a five-card suit in which to attack.

Here are three example hands you might hold when the player on your right has dealt and opened one no-trump.

(a) ♠ A Q 7 4	(b) ♠ A K J 6 5	(c) ♠ A K J 7 6 4
♡ K 8 5	♡ K 3 2	♡ Q J 8
◇ A J 2	◇ A 7 6	◇ 7 5 4
♣ Q 8 3	♣ 4 2	♣ K

Hand (a) is balanced and contains 16 high-card points. Double for penalties. You don't need very much from your partner for your side to make at least seven tricks. But exchange the queen of spades for the eight, and now you're down to 14 points so you must just pass and hope he goes down anyway. You can't pass on 14 points? Nonsense! Once you've learned to do that, you'll have learned one of the most difficult bids in bridge! Anyway, if you double, opener will know exactly where to place most of the missing points and so may well make his contract, when he'd have gone down for sure if you'd left well alone.

Hand (b) has only 15 points but you have a good suit to lead and probably two outside entries. Double, and you will be unlucky not to defeat the contract.

Holding hand (c) just bid a quiet two spades. You have no certainty that you will defeat one no-trump. Opener may have a spade stop, and you have no sure outside entry. Even if your partner holds the queen of spades you cannot be sure of more than six spade tricks, after which declarer may have the remaining seven tricks.

Opener's Partner's Action after the Penalty Double

Now we'll tell you something about what the partner of a player whose one no-trump opening has been doubled should do. You are in third seat, and partner, who has opened one no-trump, has been doubled. You'll get a nasty sinking feeling if you are sitting there holding a near Yarborough without even a five-card or longer suit to bid! At this stage in your career our advice to you is to pass unhurriedly and calmly, and keep your fingers crossed that fourth in hand may be holding something like hand (c) below and decide to bid.

When you become more expert we'll explain how you can start on a rescue effort, however weak your hand, but you may well land yourself in even worse trouble than you're in already. It can result in leaving you to play in a 4–3 fit at the two level, and it takes a really experienced player to salvage a better score than by standing the original one no-trump doubled.

If you have a five-card or better suit, bid it. The next player won't have any idea whether you are bidding on 0 or 9 points, and may be unable to double you for penalties. Your partner will, pass, and when the auction gets back to the original doubler he, too, may be uncertain as to where the balance of the points between third and fourth hands lies, so may not be able to double you for penalties either, and so you will have escaped.

With a good hand you won't, of course, think of passing. Look at the three hands below:

(a) ♠ 8 7 6	(b) ♠ Q J 8 6 3	(c) ♠ A 8 7 4
♡ 8 6 4 2	♡ 8 6	♡ K 9 4
◇ J 9 7	◇ 8 7 3	◇ Q 8 4
♣ J 5 2	♣ 6 4 2	♣ K 9 2

On hand (a) just pass and pray, as we've been explaining above.

With hand (b) bid two spades which is, we hope, what you would have done even if partner's one no-trump hadn't been doubled. Put in, say, the king of diamonds and the queen of clubs, and still just bid two spades. You probably won't be doubled, and even if you are, you might make it! How triumphant you will feel if that happens! If you are lucky enough to hold hand (c) or better, redouble with well-concealed joy. You're already in a game contract so now it's your opponents who will be on the run. You will be able to double anything they try to escape into. Don't let them off the hook by bidding two no-trumps. Remember, one no-trump doubled and redoubled is game for you!

Action by the Doubler's Partner

Next we'll look at things from the point of view of the doubler's partner. Don't forget that your partner, generally sitting immediately over the no-trump opening, has doubled for penalties and you should make every effort to leave the double undisturbed. There are just two types of hand on which you will take it out, the first being a very weak hand – say 5 points or less – and a five or six card suit – take out into your suit. No matter how weak your hand is in high-card points, don't take out partner's double without at least a five-card suit unless opener's partner has redoubled. Now you may well bid on a four-card suit in a desperate attempt to improve things for your side, though you are just as likely to be jumping out of the frying pan into the fire anyway. But to go back to taking out the double on weakness plus a five or six-card suit, how likely is your partner to choose your suit to lead? And even if he does, how are you to get in to make your tricks without entries?

We'll say more about what happens when opener's partner bids after the penalty double in a moment. Meanwhile, the other type of hand on which you should take out partner's penalty double is usually where your side is vulnerable and your opponents are not. You fear that the penalty you will get won't be big enough to compensate for the certain game and possible slam if you and your partner bid on. You must, of course, make a jump bid in your suit (1NT – Dble – Pass – 3♡, for example) to make sure that your partner doesn't pass your bid as a weakness take-out.

Sometimes you'll find it is a very difficult decision for you, particularly if you hold around 10 points in an unbalanced hand. Opener may go only one or two down in his contract when you could have made the rubber game, and yet you may well not make your four hearts, four spades, or whatever game you choose to bid, and partner will not be amused! Ah well, that's bridge, and half the fascination of this, in our opinion, best of all card games, would disappear if we all had a copper-bottomed guarantee that we should always make the right decision!

Now look at these three example hands, and decide what you would bid, fourth in hand, after an opening one no-trump doubled by your partner and passed round to you. For the purposes of this little exercise, you are vulnerable and your opponents are not, and if you think it's all very difficult, isn't that just what a weak no-trump opening is aiming to achieve?

(a) ♠ 7 3　　　　　(b) ♠ 8 6 3 2　　　　(c) ♠ 9 2
　　♡ J 9 8 7 2　　　　♡ K Q 9 4　　　　♡ J 4
　　◊ J 7 5　　　　　　◊ Q 10 9 6　　　　◊ K Q J 7 6 2
　　♣ 8 6 2　　　　　　♣ 6　　　　　　　♣ 5 4 3

With hand (a) take out the double into two hearts. Your chances of making are slim unless partner has a really strong double, but one no-trump doubled looks a very possible make. Move the two of hearts up into the spade suit, and you would pass. Just shut your eyes and pray that partner holds enough high cards to defeat one no-trump. If he hasn't, well, worse things have happened than the opponents making a doubled contract. With hand (b), pass. You have every hope of defeating declarer, and game your way is unlikely. Don't, for heaven's sake, do what one of our pupils did recently, and bid two clubs intending it for 'Stayman'. The doubler took it as a weak take-out in clubs, and passed, holding only ♣ K-4, the opponents got a super cross-ruff going and took ten tricks! Minus 500 was the score, as both sides were vulnerable, instead of plus 500 for one no-trump doubled going down two tricks. With hand (c) did you make the mistake of passing for penalties just because you held 7 points? If you did, you're a terrible gambler, betting on partner holding something like ◊ A-x-x and leading diamonds early on! That suit is almost certainly dead as far as the defence is concerned (remember you're not even on lead against the doubled contract!). Bid a quiet two diamonds and expect to make it. Of course, if your suit were a major and you top up the hand with one of the minor suit aces, you would bid three hearts or three spades, forcing partner to at least a major suit game. Give him the right cards, and there might even be a slam on.

Watch out for the rescue attempt by opener's partner. Your partner has told you he has at least a good 15 points and if you have plus 6 points and three, preferably four of the suit bid on your right, double for penalties. There is unlikely to be a game for your side, and yet you mustn't allow the others to escape undoubled. If you pass the escape effort, your partner may be unable to do anything else, just because you've told him you can't bid yourself or make another penalty double.

19
Doubling for Penalties

Doubling your opponents for penalties – and gaining a worthwhile bonus for getting them down, you hope! – adds a special dimension to the defence of a hand, and it's certainly one of the weapons you need to add to your bridge armoury as you get to be a more expert player. Do you find that your opponents are frequently out-bidding you, and are playing the hands for a small loss when the contract really belongs your way, so that all you're gaining is a measly 50 or 100 points? Then it's high time you learned to double them, and sometimes get them down heavily. You'll be surprised how soon they learn to treat you with respect, and sometimes they will even fail to bid on when the contract belongs their way.

Do you remember how we drummed into you right from the beginning the folly of making silly intervening bids? Well, now you're going to learn why, which is that good opponents will double risky overcalls and will rake in the money from reckless opponents.

Novice players never dare to double the opposition below game level because they're terrified of 'doubling them into game', 'partner how could I risk that?' So let's get two things straight in our minds right away. Firstly, opportunities to double low-level contracts, and get a good profit out of it, arise much more frequently than you are at present realising. Secondly, now and again you will double a contract, even a part-score contract, that is made. If you do, well, too bad – worse things have happened at sea, and you mustn't be deterred from doubling the next time you feel certain they can't make whatever they have bid. Nine times out of ten you will be right, so who cares about the tenth time? As we tell you over and over again, it would take all the fun out of bridge if you always had a copper-bottomed guarantee that whatever you bid would be right!

Beware of doubling the opposition's freely bid game or slam, unless your hand holds a really unpleasant surprise for declarer in the shape of sure trump tricks or really unexpectedly nasty distribution. Otherwise the probable result of your unwise double will be that, having warned declarer what to expect, he may find a way of making after all.

Remember that, at the moment, we're not talking about contested auctions, which is a very different thing. If your opponents are clearly sacrificing against your game or slam, you must either bid on or double for penalties. If you suspect you have been pushed too high, instead of bidding still one more, double and take what profit you can. Remember to listen to the auction and then to differentiate between playing tricks and defensive tricks. The ace and king of a suit bid and supported by you and your partner may not be worth even one trick in defence!

Before you read further, check to make quite sure you are clear about when your partner's double is for penalties or for take-out. Here we must just remind you that the double of an opening one no-trump bid is always intended primarily for penalties. So you, as the doubler's partner, should leave the double in unless you can see a very, very good reason for removing it.

You and your partner should treat low-level penalty doubles as co-operative. So if, for instance, the auction goes like this and you hold the North cards, give careful consideration to what South is saying.

West	North	East	South
–	1♠	2♦	Double
Pass			

Unless you are using the negative double that we mentioned in Chapter 17, partner is doubling because he thinks that your side has the balance of the points, that he doesn't much care for your spades, that he can see three tricks in his own hand, and that he has a damaging holding in diamonds.

The second point is very important – remember that the more spades you and your partner hold between you, the less likely you are to take defensive tricks in the suit, so you can expect partner to hold something like this hand.

♠ 7 2
♡ A J 9
♦ K J 8 7 5
♣ 8 7 6

If, in spite of being aware of the type of hand he holds, you are unable to agree with his idea of defending two diamonds doubled, then don't hesitate to take out the double if you wish. The example given is pretty cast-iron for reaping a good penalty, but it could be less perfect, and many players fail to make somewhat speculative low-level doubles because they don't trust their partners to take out with a hand unsuited for defence.

Now let's look at a few hands which you might hold when your right-hand opponent intervenes over your partner's opening bid and see what action you should take, and why.

(a) ♠ 10 4	(b) ♠ 5	(c) ♠ A Q J
♡ A 5 3	♡ K 10 3 2	♡ K 10 4 3
◇ J 10 4 2	◇ A J 9 6 3	◇ J 8 6 3
♣ K J 8 2	♣ Q J 7	♣ 7 4

Your partner has opened one spade and there has been an intervening bid of two diamonds. Hand (a) is the minimum on which you should make a penalty double. Many learner players would opt for bidding two no-trumps, but there is very little chance of making a game your way, and you have every hope that your hand alone will be worth three tricks – a trump, and the ace of hearts and the king of clubs – not counting what will come from partner's opening bid. If your partner leaves the double in, it's most unlikely that your right-hand opponent can make eight tricks with diamonds as trumps. If you bid no-trumps instead of doubling you will probably be exchanging a nice plus score by way of a penalty for no better than a measly part-score. Hand (b) is a super doubling hand! You have absolutely no fit for partner's spades, splendid diamonds, and honours in both unbid suits. If partner won't stand the double and removes to two spades, you will make a game try yourself with a bid of two no-trumps, but whatever the vulnerability, to defend two diamonds doubled must be most attractive to you. Hand (c) is quite the reverse. In spite of your 11 points, too many of them are in partner's suit and may be quite useless in defence. Try an immediate two no-trumps and see what develops. Yes, the clubs are a bit of a risk but partner must have something else outside his spade suit and you have no other possible call. To bid two spades would be a disastrous underbid, introducing hearts would guarantee a five-card holding and, as we've already said, to double the intervening bid of two diamonds might result in partner leaving the double in. With your points in spades the contract might even make(!) or, more likely, you will have missed the spade game.

Now let's change seats and make yourself opener, and see what action you should take after your partner's double of an intervening bid. Remember what partner is promising by his double – a shortage in your suit, a decent holding in the enemy's trumps, and a belief that his hand will produce in the region of three tricks in defence of the suit he has doubled. If you think that your hand will also produce three tricks in defence, then you should stand the double.

(a) ♠ K Q J 9 2 (b) ♠ A Q J 6 3 2 (c) ♠ A K Q 9 8 6
    ♡ J 8 3   ♡ Q J 10 7   ♡ 9 6
    ◇ 6 2   ◇ –   ◇ 10 2
    ♣ A K 3   ♣ 9 7 5   ♣ Q 7 5

The arithmetic is simple, isn't it? If you and partner expect to make six tricks between you, then the overcaller's ration will be seven at most and, therefore, he won't make his contract. After your opening bid of one spade and an intervening bid of two diamonds doubled by your partner, hand (a) should produce two tricks in the ♣ A-K, and your spades, opposite your partner's known shortage, should be good for at least one trick. The jack of hearts may help to create at least one trick between you and your partner, so naturally you will pass the double for penalties. Hand (b) is rather different. Your ♠ A-Q-J may produce two tricks, but you are not going to contribute anything else in the way of defensive tricks. Bid two hearts yourself, telling your partner clearly that you don't fancy life as a defender, and you may well find that there is a game in hearts on your way. Hand (c) is an easy one. Clearly you must take out the double into two spades, as you have no real hope of defeating two diamonds doubled if your partner's double was made on minimal values.

When considering whether or not to make a penalty double, or to pass one made by your partner, do take into account the vulnerability. If your side is vulnerable and the opposition is not, it's not much use getting them one down which, even doubled, gives you a gain of only 100 points, when you could have made a vulnerable game your way. If your own suit is long and solid and you have tricks to spare, you may be able to ignore partner's warning that he is short in your suit and still bid game in it or, with a strong balanced hand you may be able to try three no-trumps. You're not likely to have anything to speak of in your opponent's suit, but if partner's holding was good enough to double, that should produce a stop. As the opening bidder you are probably the one best able to judge when you should take out partner's double, not on weakness and because you fear the enemy contract may make, but because of what you may be missing your way.

Here is a hand from a duplicate pairs tournament to illustrate these last points.

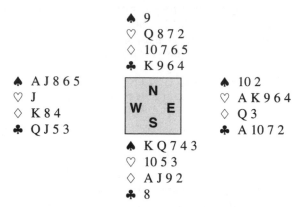

```
              ♠ 9
              ♡ Q 8 7 2
              ◇ 10 7 6 5
              ♣ K 9 6 4
♠ A J 8 6 5                      ♠ 10 2
♡ J              N               ♡ A K 9 6 4
◇ K 8 4       W     E            ◇ Q 3
♣ Q J 5 3        S               ♣ A 10 7 2
              ♠ K Q 7 4 3
              ♡ 10 5 3
              ◇ A J 9 2
              ♣ 8
```

All the East players opened one heart and the non-vulnerable South came in with one spade. Most East–West pairs went on to bid a vulnerable three no-trumps and scored +600.

Five West's opted to double the one spade intervention. This, as you can see, was questionable, as it doesn't usually pay to double a one-level contract, at which West should have been able to judge that his hand would produce four tricks. On all five occasions East passed the double, and the records show that three East-West pairs defeated the contract by only two tricks for a score of +300, and one pair was held to four tricks for +500 to East-West, still less than the 600 points for game. Only one pair managed to defeat one spade doubled by four tricks for a score of +800 points, but a defence as tight as that had to be will need you to take tranquillisers for the rest of the session!

Do remember that, when taking out a double because you think there is a game on for your side, you mustn't make a weak rebid. If you do, you'll end up with a part-score, having gained neither a game nor a sizeable penalty for your side, and your partner will not be amused! Be sure your take-out is strong, and is one that will encourage your partner to tell you more about his hand and what he has doubled on, if you aren't yet able to choose the right game for your side. It's not unknown for a partnership to bid on to a slam after an intervention, because the intervening bid has made it easier to discover that the important cards are held in exactly the right places.

We'll end this chapter by looking at one or two situations where you will want to double your opponents' freely bid contract, but do remember that not only do you warn the opposition of bad breaks but the more you have the less you can expect partner to contribute. Sitting West you hold this hand and the bidding proceeds as follows:

♠ Q J 8	West	North	East	South
♡ K J 8 2	–	–	–	1♡
◊ A J 10 9	Pass	2♣	Pass	2NT
♣ 3 2	Pass	3NT	All Pass	

Pass throughout! If you come with a take-out double partner will surely bid clubs and in this example clearly North would have redoubled your call and now the roof will fall in on you and partner! Keep very quiet and South, who has no reason to suspect that you have all the opposition's strength, is very likely to go down anyway. Double his final contract and you have given him every hint as to how to try to make it.

A good moment to double a freely bid contract is when your opponents clearly hold a misfit, but don't double too soon! Sitting West again, this time you hold this hand and the auction proceeds as below:

♠ 2	West	North	East	South
♡ Q J 8 5	Pass	1♣	1♠	2◊
◊ K 10 9 8	Pass	3♣	Pass	3◊
♣ A J 9 2	Double			

Do not be tempted to bid two no-trumps over South's two diamond call. You realise that partner has nothing much but long spades. North and South are in a forcing situation so you know South must bid again and now, when North rebids his diamonds, make your penalty double. Had he left South's three club bid in, you would have doubled that. If you make a positive call you will find yourself chalking up a minus for your side rather than the plus you have every expectation of gaining out of the opposition's misfit on this deal.

Doubling opponents who have bid freely into a game or slam requires your hand to have a really nasty surprise in store. You're West again, with these cards and the auction is as shown below:

	West	North	East	South
♠ Q 6 4				
♡ Q J 3 2	–	–	–	1NT
◇ 7 5 4 3	Pass	2♣	Pass	2♡
♣ A K	Pass	4♡	All Pass	

Don't even think of doubling South's four hearts. Left to himself he is very likely to go down, but warn him of the bad trump break and you'll tell him to finesse you for both missing trump honours. Take away your queen of spades and give yourself ♡ Q-J-10-9. Now you have only 10 points not 12, but this is where you should make a penalty double. Provided your ♣ A-K stand up, which is almost a certainty, the contract is bound to go down. If partner has a crucial card, declarer is likely to play you for it on your double.

PART II
DECLARER PLAY

20
Playing in Trump Contracts

Handling Trumps

You've come to the point now when you need to give more thought to the handling of your trumps when you're playing in a suit contract. After all, you've chosen to play with a certain suit as trumps rather than in no-trumps because you have discovered that you have more of that suit between you and your partner than your opponents have, so it's up to you to make the best possible use of them. It's not a golden rule that you should draw all the opponents' trumps just as soon as you win a trick – if you do, you'll soon find yourself sleeping on the embankment, as the old saying goes. You're just as likely to end up there by making it a rule to draw trumps and then, and only then, stopping to plan how to get the rest of the tricks you need. Nine times out of ten you'll wish you hadn't been in such an unholy hurry because there was something you should have done, especially with dummy's trumps, before you drew them. So here's the correct golden rule for you – *never draw all the trumps before making quite sure you don't want to use them in other ways first*. Here's a quick reminder of the main uses for trumps.

Uses for Trumps

1 To ruff the opponents' winners in a suit in which you or dummy are void.

2 To cross from hand to hand when you want to do something else – that is to use trumps as entries.

3 To ruff your own losers, usually with the shorter holding of trumps.

4 To establish a side suit, either in your own hand or in dummy, on which to discard losers.

5 To 'strip' a hand preparing for an end-play.

Sometimes you'll find that you can afford to draw one or even two rounds of trumps before setting about the rest of the business of making the hand. On other occasions to touch trumps could prove fatal. Look at the following full deal which illustrates the common technique of 'cross-ruffing'. You are South playing in four hearts against the lead of the king of clubs.

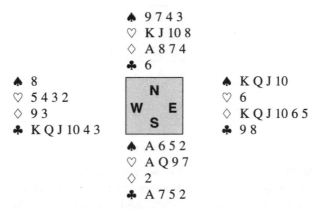

♠ 9 7 4 3
♡ K J 10 8
◇ A 8 7 4
♣ 6

♠ 8
♡ 5 4 3 2
◇ 9 3
♣ K Q J 10 4 3

♠ K Q J 10
♡ 6
◇ K Q J 10 6 5
♣ 9 8

♠ A 6 5 2
♡ A Q 9 7
◇ 2
♣ A 7 5 2

You have splendid trumps but outside the heart suit there are precisely three winners – the three aces. The seven more tricks you need can come from using each one of your trumps separately. If you want ten tricks don't forget to take your ace of spades early on while you are busy cross-ruffing. Otherwise West will discard his singleton spade on the third round of diamonds and ruff your ace of spades, and if he then gets off lead with another of his small trumps you will actually go down in your four heart contract!

Now let's look at a few hands to illustrate what we've said above. In each case we've given you just your own hand and dummy first, so that you can work out your plan of play before you study the full deal.

Ruffing in Dummy

♠ K 7 3
♡ 10 7 4
◇ 8 7 5 4 2
♣ A 2

```
      N
  W       E
      S
```

♠ A 6 5 4
♡ K Q J 9 6
◇ A K
♣ 5 4

You are South, declarer in four hearts and West leads the king of clubs.

Study dummy and count up your winners. There are five top winners outside the trump suit and four trump winners in your own hand, so you need only to look for a tenth trick. Did you think of setting up the diamonds? Forget that one, as you just don't have enough entries to dummy even if both the diamonds and trumps break well for you. What about the spade suit, then? Well, it might break 3-3 (or it might not!) – but now you are on the right lines. Even if the spades break 4-2, and by now you know enough to know that this is the more likely lie of six missing cards, you can still make your contract by ruffing one in dummy, but this has to be done before you draw trumps. Why?

Trumps can't break better than 3-2, so the three rounds needed to draw them will mean you haven't a trump left in dummy to ruff with. So win the ace of clubs, cash the ace and king of diamonds in case either opponent is able to discard one on a third round of spades, and cash the king of spades, then the ace of spades, and then play a losing spade. If all follow, which means spades have broken 3–3, you won't need the ruff. If not, as soon as you get back into your own hand, probably after the defence has cashed a club trick, lead your last spade, and be sure to ruff it with the ten of hearts, because East didn't follow to the third round of spades. So now he will either over-ruff with the ace of hearts, which is a winner anyway, or you have your tenth trick and can set about drawing trumps yourself.

```
                ♠ K 7 3
                ♡ 10 7 4
                ◇ 8 7 5 4 2
                ♣ A 2
  ♠ Q J 8 2    ┌─────────┐   ♠ 10 9
  ♡ 3 2        │    N    │   ♡ A 8 5
  ◇ J 9        │ W     E │   ◇ Q 10 6 3
  ♣ K Q J 8 3  │    S    │   ♣ 10 9 7 6
                └─────────┘
                ♠ A 6 5 4
                ♡ K Q J 9 6
                ◇ A K
                ♣ 5 4
```

Playing for a 3-2 Trump Break

```
                ♠ 6 2
                ♡ K 6 4 2
                ◇ A 8 6 3
                ♣ A 6 4

              ┌─────────┐
              │    N    │
              │ W     E │
              │    S    │
              └─────────┘
                ♠ A 8 5 3
                ♡ A 7 5 3
                ◇ K J 5
                ♣ K 3
```

Again you and your partner have bid to four hearts, and though you certainly
have the points for game, when West leads the queen of spades and dummy
goes down, prospects look a bit thin. Three no-trumps might have been a
better spot but you're going to have to make the best you can of four hearts.

How did you get on?

Your top tricks add up to seven, one spade, two hearts, two diamonds and
two clubs, but the rest will have to come from the jack of diamonds and
little trumps, so you plan to try to ruff spades in dummy. Yes, the right idea,
but do you duck a spade, win the probable continuation, and then try to ruff
two spades? The trouble with that idea is that dummy's trumps are so small
that you're likely to be overruffed by East. So what should you do?

It's all a question of timing, which means doing the right thing at the right moment. After ducking the spade and winning the continuation, you must cash the ace and king of hearts before trying for any ruffs at all. If the trumps break 4-1 you've next to no chance of making this contract, so cross your fingers and pray for the more probable 3-2 break. If both opponents follow to two rounds of trumps, now lead a spade to dummy to ruff, cash your top clubs, ruff a club and ruff your last spade. Yes, of course someone will over-ruff sometime, but he will do so with a master trump, and you will have no trouble in coping with whatever he returns, and proceeding on your cross-ruff lines, losing only a trump, a spade, and a diamond. Look at the defending hands, and you will see how it all works out.

```
                      ♠ 6 2
                      ♡ K 6 4 2
                      ◇ A 8 6 3
                      ♣ A 6 4
    ♠ Q J 10 9 4         N         ♠ K 7
    ♡ Q 9 8                        ♡ J 10
    ◇ Q 4         W         E      ◇ 10 9 7 2
    ♣ 9 8 7            S           ♣ Q J 10 5 2
                      ♠ A 8 5 3
                      ♡ A 7 5 3
                      ◇ K J 5
                      ♣ K 3
```

Here's another one to show you how and when to draw trumps. It's really the same hand as the previous one, with the same number of high-card points, but set out a little differently and needing a slightly different line of play:

```
                      ♠ K 6
                      ♡ 9 6 4 2
                      ◇ A 8 4
                      ♣ A 8 6 3
                          N
                      W         E
                          S
                      ♠ A 7 4 2
                      ♡ A 8 5 3
                      ◇ K 2
                      ♣ K J 2
```

Again, you are in four hearts, and West leads the queen of spades, so how do you wrap up ten tricks this time?

If you study the hands carefully you will see that the number of high cards is exactly the same but that you now have the king of spades instead of the trump king, and again you are going to need a kindly trump break. Again you are very likely to be over-ruffed unless you draw some of the enemy's teeth, but if you play the ace of hearts and another, the defender who wins may have the last trump and be unkind enough to draw to a third round. Now you won't be able to come to ten tricks by playing on a cross-ruff. Did you spot it? It's a duck on the first round of trumps. Now win whatever is returned, cash the ace of hearts and continue to cross-ruff as on the previous hand. This plan will work on the 3-2 trump break. We haven't put in the defensive hands this time: try arranging them between East and West any way you like and this line of play works, provided the trumps behave.

Ruffing with Poor Trumps in the Long Holding

This last one is really rather a horrid little hand to play, and if you go slap-bang after the trumps you'll lose control and end up with about four tricks. Take it quietly and look carefully at the trump position, because it's from trumps that your tricks must come.

♠ 10 6 5
♡ K J 4 3 2
◊ 8 7 4
♣ K 3

♠ A K 4 3 2
♡ —
◊ 10 5 3
♣ A J 7 5 2

The bidding has gone one Club from you, who dealt yourself the South cards, one heart from your partner, one spade from you and no bid from your partner. The lead is a small heart, and you view dummy with some misgivings! There are losers all over the place, and you can only count four certain tricks.

What plan did you eventually make? Maybe you decided to try to establish the clubs but they are likely to break 4-2 and dummy's trumps are too small for you not to expect to be over-ruffed. What about ruffing hearts in your own hand? Not a purposeless ruff, but done with intent.

On the opening lead you play the jack of hearts which is covered by East's queen and you ruff in your own hand. Why the jack of hearts and not the king, do we hear you asking?

Well, West would be more likely to lead away from the queen of hearts than from the ace and you might strike lucky. However, as the cards lie you might just as well have played a low one, but you had to try. Now you have five tricks. If you cash the ♠ A-K at this point you are scuppered for certain if the suit doesn't break, so test the clubs first. Lead low to the king of clubs and return a low heart to ruff in hand. Next try cashing the ace of clubs and when it holds you have six tricks. Now lead a low club and when West follows suit, ruff high in dummy, or at least as high as you can, using the ten of spades. This gives you two chances for your seventh trick if East either follows suit with a club or can't over-ruff the ten. As it happens you can now ruff a third heart in hand, and a fourth club in dummy (after cashing one high trump) but this is just luck as the cards lie.

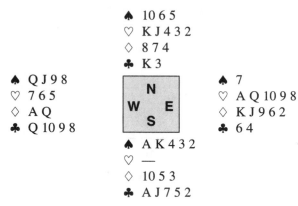

```
                 ♠ 10 6 5
                 ♡ K J 4 3 2
                 ◇ 8 7 4
                 ♣ K 3
   ♠ Q J 9 8          N          ♠ 7
   ♡ 7 6 5      W         E      ♡ A Q 10 9 8
   ◇ A Q            S            ◇ K J 9 6 2
   ♣ Q 10 9 8                    ♣ 6 4
                 ♠ A K 4 3 2
                 ♡ —
                 ◇ 10 5 3
                 ♣ A J 7 5 2
```

Suit Establishment

♠ J 2
♡ K 9 8 4 3
◇ A 7 4
♣ Q 5 2

```
      N
  W       E
      S
```

♠ A K Q 10 9 4
♡ A 5
◇ Q 8 3
♣ 9 6

You and partner have bid to an excellent contract of four spades, but the lead is the jack of clubs and inevitably the defence take the first two tricks, and East returns a third round hoping that his partner can overruff you. Of course you trump in with nine, and sit down and plan.

How did you get on? You have nine top tricks and if the king of diamonds is favourably placed, you can score the queen of diamonds for your tenth trick. But this is only a 50-50 chance – can you see a better one? Yes, if the hearts break no worse than 4-2 the thirteenth can be established for a diamond discard. So this is a better plan – but don't draw the trumps first or you will be in trouble for entries to dummy. At trick four, cash the ace of hearts and then cross to dummy with the king of hearts. When this stands up, all is well. Now play a heart to ruff in your own hand. East discards but no matter. Return to dummy with the jack of spades and ruff another heart. Now comes the time to draw trumps and return to dummy with the ace of diamonds to discard a diamond loser on the established heart.

The full deal is shown below.

You might like to consider what would have happened if East had switched to a diamond at trick three, or if declarer had drawn trumps after ruffing the third round of clubs.

```
                        ♠ J 2
                        ♡ K 9 8 4 3
                        ◇ A 7 4
                        ♣ Q 5 2
    ♠ 8 7 6                              ♠ 5 3
    ♡ Q J 7 2          ┌─────────┐      ♡ 10 6
    ◇ K J 10 5         │    N    │      ◇ 9 6 2
    ♣ J 10          W  │ W     E │  E   ♣ A K 8 7 4 3
                       │    S    │
                       └─────────┘
                        ♠ A K Q 10 9 4
                        ♡ A 5
                        ◇ Q 8 3
                        ♣ 9 6
```

21
More About Playing in Trump Contracts

The hands that we gave you to play in the previous chapter concentrated on the way you handled your trump suit. The deals that follow illustrate some of the other techniques that you must master if you are to succeed whenever it is possible to make your contract.

Unblocking

♠ 3 2
♡ A 9 8
◇ Q 7 2
♣ J 9 4 3 2

♠ A Q J 10 7 4
♡ K 6 2
◇ A J
♣ A 6

This time you are South, playing in four spades against which West leads the queen of hearts. Don't look at the following text, and plan the play for ten tricks. Don't worry about overtricks – we just want to be sure you make the contract.

Like so many contracts, this one depends solely on your play at trick one! If you won the opening lead in dummy in order to take a trump, or even a diamond finesse, you went down, and all for the lack of a little thought! The ace of hearts is your only entry to dummy, and must be kept until you really need it. A quick count of top tricks gives you five spades, two hearts, and the two minor suit aces – nine in all. The tenth could come from the trump suit or from the diamonds, you will say to yourself. Making all six trumps in your own hand depends not only on the king of spades being on your right, but on it being ♠ K-x precisely too, or you won't be able to pick it up, as you can only finesse once. So if six spade tricks are highly unlikely, surely the diamond suit must be the better bet, because it can't fail to produce two tricks wherever the king of diamonds is.

We do hope you worked out all this easily, but did you get to the difficult bit? It's no good establishing the queen of diamonds in dummy as a winner if you can't get at it! So what you must do is win trick one with the king of hearts in your own hand and immediately play the ace of diamonds followed by the jack of diamonds. Did you, we wonder? Look at the full deal below:

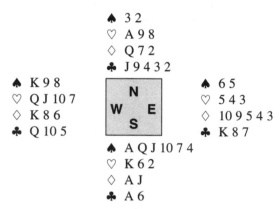

```
            ♠  3 2
            ♡  A 9 8
            ◇  Q 7 2
            ♣  J 9 4 3 2
♠ K 9 8                      ♠  6 5
♡ Q J 10 7      N            ♡  5 4 3
◇ K 8 6    W       E         ◇  10 9 5 4 3
♣ Q 10 5        S            ♣  K 8 7
            ♠  A Q J 10 7 4
            ♡  K 6 2
            ◇  A J
            ♣  A 6
```

Both the spade and diamond kings, are offside, but you still make the contract because when West wins with the king of diamonds at trick 3 he will probably continue with the jack of hearts, but you are in control. Win in dummy and discard your losing heart on the queen of diamonds. You are even ready now to try for an overtrick by taking the trump finesse and hoping for precisely ♠ K-x on your right. In any event you must now get home with your ten tricks.

The moral of this story is that yet again you mustn't feel you must rush to draw trumps just as soon as you win a trick. Here you delayed touching trumps until trick six, and you still made the contract.

Creating a 'Parking Place'

♠ J 10 3
♡ Q J 6
◇ K 10 9
♣ A K 8 5

♠ 7 6 4
♡ K 10 7 5 3 2
◇ Q
♣ 7 6 2

Just for a change here you are in a part-score of two hearts, partner having opened one no-trump. West leads the queen of clubs.

The title should have given you a clue to this problem! In low-level contracts it's often easier to count your sure losers rather than your winners and here we have rather a lot – potentially one too many, in fact. The defenders will take their ♠ A-K-Q, ace of diamonds and ace of trumps, but you feel quite happy there won't be a club loser because you can discard it on the king of diamonds. Well, yes, that might have worked had the defenders not found the killing lead to scotch that plan. There's only one way to get home and that is if you played a low diamond to your queen of diamonds at trick two and did not touch trumps. Now when the defence continue with another club you can win in dummy and discard your last club on the king of diamonds. Now you can tackle trumps – your contract is on ice.

The full deal was as below and you can see just what would have happened if you had played a trump at trick 2.

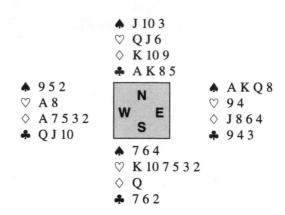

```
              ♠ J 10 3
              ♡ Q J 6
              ◇ K 10 9
              ♣ A K 8 5
♠ 9 5 2                      ♠ A K Q 8
♡ A 8          N            ♡ 9 4
◇ A 7 5 3 2   W   E         ◇ J 8 6 4
♣ Q J 10       S            ♣ 9 4 3
              ♠ 7 6 4
              ♡ K 10 7 5 3 2
              ◇ Q
              ♣ 7 6 2
```

Cutting Communications

```
              ♠ J 10 9
              ♡ 8 6
              ◇ A K J 10 9
              ♣ 7 6 4
```

```
              ♠ A Q 8 7 6
              ♡ A 9
              ◇ Q 5 3
              ♣ K 9 2
```

Your contract is four spades and West leads the queen of hearts. Easy – or not?

This contract is often given by the defence and declarer never knows that he risked going down. At trick one all looks fine, just a heart to lose and the ace of clubs and perhaps the trump finesse will work and we'll get eleven tricks. Did you win ace of hearts, cross to dummy with a diamond and take the spade finesse? Well, if you did, then when it lost West could put East in with king of hearts (you knew he had it) for the fatal switch to the queen of clubs. When you look at the full deal you'll see just how that can happen. Unlucky you feel – we've put everything in the wrong place? No, poor play on your part. Just let the queen of hearts hold the first trick (unless the defence is smart enough to put on the king when, of course, you must play your ace). Now it doesn't matter if the trump finesse fails for East can never get in, and dummy's diamond suit will provide for two club discards.

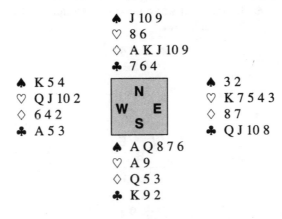

```
                    ♠ J 10 9
                    ♡ 8 6
                    ◇ A K J 10 9
                    ♣ 7 6 4
  ♠ K 5 4              N            ♠ 3 2
  ♡ Q J 10 2      W       E        ♡ K 7 5 4 3
  ◇ 6 4 2             S            ◇ 8 7
  ♣ A 5 3                          ♣ Q J 10 8
                    ♠ A Q 8 7 6
                    ♡ A 9
                    ◇ Q 5 3
                    ♣ K 9 2
```

Ducking

Ducking, or holding up, is a play that to the average declarer is reserved for playing in no-trumps. The above hand was an example of declarer ducking, hoping to keep a dangerous defender out of the lead. Here is another example of a strategic duck. See how you do with it.

```
                    ♠ K 7 4
                    ♡ 6 5 3
                    ◇ A 4 3
                    ♣ A Q J 4
                        N
                    W       E
                        S
                    ♠ A 10 9 5 2
                    ♡ A J 4
                    ◇ K 9 5
                    ♣ 10 9
```

You are in four spades, after partner's opening bid of one no-trump and you get the lead of the king of hearts.

A check on winners and losers shows that at least one trump must be lost, a club if the finesse is wrong, and the defence have unerringly attacked one of your weak suits. Did you win the ace of hearts at trick one, and finesse trumps towards West to safeguard your jack of hearts and pray for the clubs to behave? If you did it was a good try, but not good enough as you can see from the full deal below.

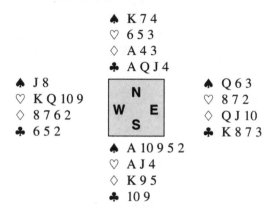

$$
\begin{array}{c}
\spadesuit\ K\,7\,4 \\
\heartsuit\ 6\,5\,3 \\
\diamondsuit\ A\,4\,3 \\
\clubsuit\ A\,Q\,J\,4
\end{array}
$$

$$
\begin{array}{l}
\spadesuit\ J\,8 \\
\heartsuit\ K\,Q\,10\,9 \\
\diamondsuit\ 8\,7\,6\,2 \\
\clubsuit\ 6\,5\,2
\end{array}
\qquad
\begin{array}{l}
\spadesuit\ Q\,6\,3 \\
\heartsuit\ 8\,7\,2 \\
\diamondsuit\ Q\,J\,10 \\
\clubsuit\ K\,8\,7\,3
\end{array}
$$

$$
\begin{array}{c}
\spadesuit\ A\,10\,9\,5\,2 \\
\heartsuit\ A\,J\,4 \\
\diamondsuit\ K\,9\,5 \\
\clubsuit\ 10\,9
\end{array}
$$

East gets in with the king of clubs and returns a heart through your ♡ J-6 and there's still the trump queen to lose. The winning play was to duck the king of hearts at trick one! What does West do now? If he continues with another heart he gives you two heart tricks, and this he knows from his partner's discouraging two of hearts.

So he switches to a minor suit. If to clubs, take the finesse. East wins and returns a heart but now you go up with ace of hearts, cash the ace and king of spades and run the clubs until someone ruffs in. If West plays a diamond at trick 2, win in hand and again cash the trump tops before taking the club finesse yourself.

This particular piece of declarer play declarer play is known as the Bath Coup, a play discovered in the days of whist in the watering spa of Bath.

Finessing

The next two hands concern the gentle art of finessing – something every beginner is taught to do and then has to learn when not to do it! Try this deal.

♠ A Q J 10
♡ Q 9 6 2
◇ 5 4 3
♣ A 3

♠ 7
♡ A K J 10 8
◇ K 6 2
♣ 9 8 7 6

You are playing in four hearts and receive the passive lead of a small trump. How do you plan the play?

Did you draw trumps and then take the spade finesse? In fact it loses and back comes the fatal queen of diamonds through your king and down you go. Unlucky? Well, suppose the spade finesse had been right? You can't take it again so you would have to lose to the king of spades eventually – so don't take the risk of it being wrong. Draw trumps, play to the ace of spades and return the queen of spades for a 'ruffing finesse'.

This means that if the queen of spades is covered by the king you can ruff it, and return to dummy to discard two diamonds on the now established spades. If it's not covered, discard a diamond. West may win, but what harm can he do you now your king of diamonds is now safe from attack? This ruffing finesse acts as an avoidance play and when, on different deals, you have to decide between a simple finesse or a ruffing finesse, your choice will often be based on knowing which defender you cannot afford to allow into the lead.

Here is the full deal:

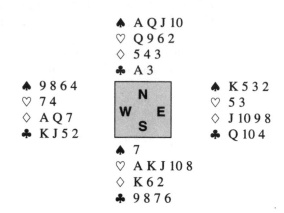

```
              ♠ A Q J 10
              ♡ Q 9 6 2
              ◇ 5 4 3
              ♣ A 3
♠ 9 8 6 4                      ♠ K 5 3 2
♡ 7 4          N               ♡ 5 3
◇ A Q 7    W       E           ◇ J 10 9 8
♣ K J 5 2      S               ♣ Q 10 4
              ♠ 7
              ♡ A K J 10 8
              ◇ K 6 2
              ♣ 9 8 7 6
```

This next, and last hand in this chapter is also to do with finessing.

```
              ♠ 10 8 5 3 2
              ♡ A Q 7 5
              ◇ 8
              ♣ 7 6 2
```

```
              ♠ A Q 9 7 4
              ♡ 8 6
              ◇ A K Q J
              ♣ Q 10
```

Against your four spade contract West starts with the ace and king of clubs and switches to the four of hearts. How do you tackle the hand?

It looks as if there are inevitably two clubs to lose and that either the heart finesse or the spade finesse must work to allow you home with ten tricks. You know that finesses have a 50% chance of being right so surely you can't be so unlucky as to find two wrong on the same hand, you feel, and anyway West's four of hearts looks like low away from an honour, so you put on the queen. Bingo, the king snaps it up on your right and back comes the club, and then the wretched spade finesse was wrong, too. 'Sorry, partner, nothing I could do'. Oh yes, there was. Don't finesse at all, neither trumps nor hearts! Play the ace of hearts at trick 2, and then the ace of spades. After all, you have ten trumps and maybe the king is singleton. No matter when it isn't, leave trumps alone. Run your beautiful diamonds discarding dummy's two clubs. Providing the hand left with the king of spades has at least two diamonds, your plan works. Look at the full deal, now. So obvious when we can see all four hands, isn't it!

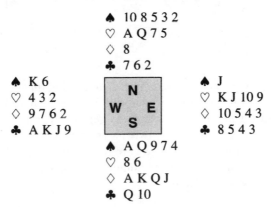

```
                 ♠ 10 8 5 3 2
                 ♡ A Q 7 5
                 ◇ 8
                 ♣ 7 6 2
   ♠ K 6              N              ♠ J
   ♡ 4 3 2                           ♡ K J 10 9
   ◇ 9 7 6 2      W       E          ◇ 10 5 4 3
   ♣ A K J 9          S              ♣ 8 5 4 3
                 ♠ A Q 9 7 4
                 ♡ 8 6
                 ◇ A K Q J
                 ♣ Q 10
```

We hope you enjoyed trying your skills with the deals featured in these last two chapters. Now try yourself out at playing in no-trumps in the next two chapters.

22
Playing a Hand in No-Trumps

No-trump play is more demanding than playing in a trump contract because if you lose control of a hand and the defence have lots of winners to cash, you won't have a chance to regain control by trumping in. However, there are various known ploys to help you and we shall be explaining the principal ones by way of the hands which follow. Again we give you first your own hand and dummy for you to make your own plan, and follow up with the full deal.

Rule of Seven

This is a very helpful rule to master. It only applies in no-trump play when you are attacked in a suit in which you have only one stopper, or sometimes two stoppers but know that you are likely to lose the lead twice before you can get home in your contract. It works like this. Add together the number of cards you hold between your own hand and dummy in the suit in which you have been attacked and take that number from seven. The answer is the number of times you need to hold up. Its commonest use is when you have just the lone ace in a suit, and you want to know how soon to play it. If you have three to the ace in your own hand and a small doubleton in dummy, the equation is $3 + 2 = 5$, taken away from $7 = 2$. So duck twice and win the third round. Why? Well it's all about how a suit will break. You have five cards, so the defenders have eight. The likely break of these eight is five and three, with the hand that has led, if it started with a small card, having the five-card holding.

By ducking the first two rounds you run his partner out of the suit, and then you will try to keep the dangerous hand off lead by using all your skills at avoidance play. If, facing your A-x-x you had x-x-x in dummy, you would say, $3 + 3 = 6$, taken away from $7 = 1$. So duck once and win the second round of the suit. If the seven cards in the opponents' hands are breaking four and three, you can only lose three tricks in it, and if they are breaking five and two, then you have already cut communications by holding up once.

Don't apply the Rule of Seven too slavishly. Sometimes it must be ignored. Suppose you are even worse off in another suit – don't give them a chance to find that one next! There is also a danger of a fatal switch if you duck to the wrong hand. There may be blocking possibilities, too. Each case must be considered individually. Have a look at the following hand and see how you think it should be played.

♠ A 7 4
♡ K 10
♢ Q J 10 9 8 2
♣ K 8

♠ K 5 2
♡ A Q J
♢ 6 5 3
♣ A 10 9 7

The lead against your three no-trump contract is the queen of spades which you have no difficulty in reading as the top of a sequence.

A count of top tricks gives you seven, with only the ♢ A-K to lose, so did you decide not to waste time, and with two stops in spades to win the first round and start to establish the diamonds? After all, with two stops it's always possible to duck the next round. If your thinking went like that you blew this beautiful contract! When you lost the first diamond another spade came back, you ducked but the suit was continued and now the wretched defender with the long spades produced the other top diamond and cashed two spade tricks. Bad luck? No, bad management and failure to use the Rule of Seven, which tells you to duck the first time and win the second. Now, provided both diamond honours are not in the hand with the five spades, you are safe. See how it works out in the full diagram.

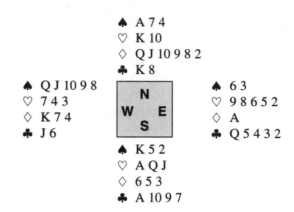

```
              ♠ A 7 4
              ♡ K 10
              ◇ Q J 10 9 8 2
              ♣ K 8
♠ Q J 10 9 8              ♠ 6 3
♡ 7 4 3                   ♡ 9 8 6 5 2
◇ K 7 4                   ◇ A
♣ J 6                     ♣ Q 5 4 3 2
              ♠ K 5 2
              ♡ A Q J
              ◇ 6 5 3
              ♣ A 10 9 7
```

Here's the next one for you to try:

```
              ♠ A 7 4
              ♡ Q 2
              ◇ 10 9 2
              ♣ A K J 9 6



              ♠ K Q 6
              ♡ K 7 5
              ◇ A Q J 5
              ♣ 10 7 3
```

You are South, declarer in three no-trumps, against which West leads the four of hearts. You play dummy's queen of hearts which holds the trick. Now don't read on before you have made your plan for nine tricks. Don't forget to work out the meaning of the card led!

Did you wonder why we played the queen of hearts at trick one? Our plan showed that we had a chance of making two heart tricks if the lead was away from the ace, as the Rule of Eleven told us it probably was. When the queen of hearts held, this dictated whether we established dummy's clubs or declarer's diamonds to make the contract. After that queen held we now have seven top tricks. Either clubs or diamonds will produce two more. However, we do not have the luxury of going for the clubs, the longest suit, because the finesse, if it loses, will allow East, who is now the danger hand, to return a heart through the king and West will take his four heart tricks. It is totally safe at trick two to run the ten of diamonds. If West wins he cannot attack hearts without conceding a trick to our king.

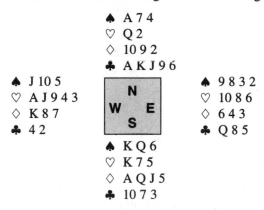

```
                    ♠ A 7 4
                    ♡ Q 2
                    ◇ 10 9 2
                    ♣ A K J 9 6
   ♠ J 10 5                        ♠ 9 8 3 2
   ♡ A J 9 4 3         N           ♡ 10 8 6
   ◇ K 8 7        W        E        ◇ 6 4 3
   ♣ 4 2              S           ♣ Q 8 5
                    ♠ K Q 6
                    ♡ K 7 5
                    ◇ A Q J 5
                    ♣ 10 7 3
```

Are you wondering what this hand has to do with the Rule of Seven? It has a lot to do with it if the cards lie differently. The king and queen of hearts between them constitute our one certain stop. If it had turned out that the lead was from five to the knave then East would have killed dummy's queen of hearts with his ace, to unblock, and you would have held up your king of hearts to the third round (Rule of Seven). Now, of course, you would take the club finesse and when it lost to East, then either he would be out of hearts, and could not get his partner back in, or the suit would have broken harmlessly 4-4. Pencil the ace of hearts in on your right and move the six of hearts to West. When you lose to queen of clubs, East will switch to diamonds to try to get his partner in. Beware! Go straight up with the ace of diamonds and run for home.

Entries

It's no good establishing a suit in your own hand or in dummy, and then finding that you've left yourself no way in to cash your winners. Planning becomes even more essential on these types of hands especially when faced at trick one with a choice of where to win a trick. As always, example hands for you to practise on before you see the full deal make life easier. Try your planning foresight on this one:

♠ 6 5
♡ A 7 5
♢ 5 3
♣ A J 10 9 8 4

♠ A J 7 2
♡ K 6 2
♢ A K 7 4 2
♣ K

To your contract of three no-trumps West leads the queen of hearts.

Firstly, did you see the play to trick one as a Rule of Seven situation? Well, it would probably not do any harm to duck as West will almost certainly play another heart, but a spade switch before you have flushed out the queen of clubs could be awkward. It's better on this occasion to win, but were you careful to win with your own king and leave the ace in dummy as an entry to the clubs? We're sure you were. Now, did you cash the king of clubs and cross to dummy with the ace of hearts to play the ace of clubs – and, oh dear, the the queen of clubs didn't drop and now all dummy's club tricks were wasted? No, of course you didn't! You saw that this play was very unlikely to work, and you carefully overtook your king of clubs with the ace (ignoring dummy's incredulous expression when told to play the ace!) and continued leading clubs until someone played the queen. Now all was plain sailing. You had control of spades and diamonds, and the ace of hearts was sitting there as an entry to the good clubs.

Here is the full deal:

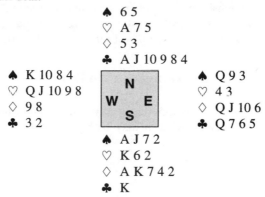

```
                    ♠ 6 5
                    ♡ A 7 5
                    ◇ 5 3
                    ♣ A J 10 9 8 4
  ♠ K 10 8 4           N            ♠ Q 9 3
  ♡ Q J 10 9 8                      ♡ 4 3
  ◇ 9 8           W       E         ◇ Q J 10 6
  ♣ 3 2                 S           ♣ Q 7 6 5
                    ♠ A J 7 2
                    ♡ K 6 2
                    ◇ A K 7 4 2
                    ♣ K
```

Here's another hand with an entry problem for you to try yourself out on:

```
                    ♠ A 8 7 3
                    ♡ A J
                    ◇ Q 3
                    ♣ A 8 7 5 2
```

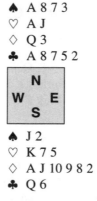

```
                    ♠ J 2
                    ♡ K 7 5
                    ◇ A J 10 9 8 2
                    ♣ Q 6
```

The led against your three no-trumps is the four of hearts.

Nice kind lead, isn't it. Fourth best away from the queen you're sure, and so you finesse dummy's jack. When East produces the queen you duck, and a second heart removes the ace from dummy. Well, that doesn't matter, does it, because it's in our hand that we want the entry for the diamonds. So now comes the queen of diamonds which holds, followed by the three of diamonds to your eight which also holds but, alas, West discards. Disaster! We cash the ace of diamonds and concede to East's king of diamonds and he switches to a club. The defence very meanly refuses to touch hearts again and you go to bed with all your beautiful diamonds, going at least one down. Unlucky? Not at all, you were too greedy at trick 1. All you had to do was play your ace of hearts and play on diamonds until you lost to the king. Now the opposition couldn't prevent you overtaking your jack of hearts with your king to cash all the winning diamonds. This was an unblocking play and another example of refusing to take a finesse.

Too Dangerous to Duck

Having stressed to you the importance of ducking in no-trump contracts, now we have to consider when it may be highly inadvisable! Here's an example.

♠ A J 5
♡ A 5
◇ Q 10 9 6 3
♣ 6 3 2

♠ Q 9 7
♡ K Q 7 2
◇ K J 8 5
♣ A Q

The contract is, once again, three no-trumps and the lead is the four of spades.

Did the play look nice and straightforward to you? Two certain stops in the enemy suit and just the ace of diamonds to clear for ten tricks, and the club finesse in reserve for a possible eleventh. Well, that's exactly the way it works out – provided you refused the tempting finesse at trick one, went up with the ace of spades and attacked diamonds. But if you got greedy and played low in dummy at trick one, East gets in with his king of spades and, of course, doesn't play his partner's suit back to him. He switches to the jack of clubs, you cover with the queen in hopes, but West wins with the king of clubs, abandons his own spades and drives out the ace of clubs and then when you have to give up a trick to the ace of diamonds, three more club tricks down your ice-cold contract. See it all set out below.

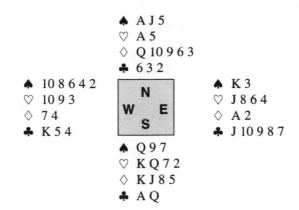

                    ♠ A J 5
                    ♡ A 5
                    ◊ Q 10 9 6 3
                    ♣ 6 3 2
    ♠ 10 8 6 4 2   ♠ K 3
    ♡ 10 9 3   N   ♡ J 8 6 4
    ◊ 7 4   W   E   ◊ A 2
    ♣ K 5 4   S   ♣ J 10 9 8 7
                    ♠ Q 9 7
                    ♡ K Q 7 2
                    ◊ K J 8 5
                    ♣ A Q

Playing in three no-trumps on the deal below you receive the lead of the
two of spades, on which you play low from dummy and East contributes
the queen.

                    ♠ 9 7 3
                    ♡ J 6
                    ◊ K Q 10 8 4
                    ♣ Q J 3
                       N
                    W   E
                       S
                    ♠ A 10 4
                    ♡ A 8 5
                    ◊ J 9 7
                    ♣ A K 4 2

Did you apply the Rule of Seven and duck? If you did you forgot two
things, one was the Rule of Eleven, which told you that the spades were
divided 4-3 and that you couldn't cut communications therefore, and the
second was that a heart lead would have been worse than the spade you
actually received. Take your ace of spades and knock out the ace of
diamonds. Now the defenders take their three spade tricks but the rest are
yours. Study the full deal and you will see that any reasonable player in the
East seat will accept his spade trick, and switch to the king of hearts
confident that he has your contract beaten – and so he has!

Yes, the cards are lying very badly for you, but why take the risk of the
fatal heart switch.

```
                    ♠ 9 7 3
                    ♡ J 6
                    ◇ K Q 10 8 4
                    ♣ Q J 3
  ♠ K J 5 2      ┌──────────┐      ♠ Q 8 6
  ♡ 7 4 3 2      │    N     │      ♡ K Q 10 9
  ◇ 6 5          │ W     E  │      ◇ A 3 2
  ♣ 10 9 8       │    S     │      ♣ 7 6 5
                 └──────────┘
                    ♠ A 10 4
                    ♡ A 8 5
                    ◇ J 9 7
                    ♣ A K 4 2
```

23
More About No-Trump Play

When to Cover a High Card

One of the bits of helpful advice freely offered to you by your friends when you first take up this game is 'always cover an honour with an honour' but they forget to complete the saying with 'when there is a hope of gain for your side'.

Here is a deal to show how wrong this advice is if the saying is not completed.

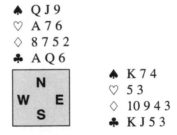

♠ Q J 9
♡ A 7 6
♢ 8 7 5 2
♣ A Q 6

♠ K 7 4
♡ 5 3
♢ 10 9 4 3
♣ K J 5 3

After South has opened with a strong two hearts, West leads the king of diamonds at trick one against the final contract of six no-trumps. Declarer wins in hand with the ace and plays the king of hearts and a heart to the ace, your partner following to both of them. When declarer plays the queen of spades from dummy is it right to cover with your king?

We hope that, right on top of the helpful advice we gave you in the opening paragraph of this chapter, you did not put on the king of spades. Every harm will be done if you cover because declarer will now be able to finesse against your partner's ten of spades. This is the full deal:

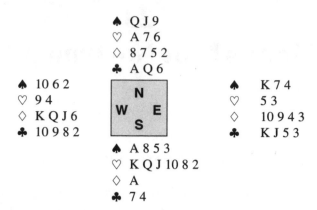

```
                    ♠ Q J 9
                    ♡ A 7 6
                    ◇ 8 7 5 2
                    ♣ A Q 6
  ♠ 10 6 2         ┌─────────┐      ♠ K 7 4
  ♡ 9 4            │    N    │      ♡ 5 3
  ◇ K Q J 6        │ W     E │      ◇ 10 9 4 3
  ♣ 10 9 8 2       │    S    │      ♣ K J 5 3
                   └─────────┘
                    ♠ A 8 5 3
                    ♡ K Q J 10 8 2
                    ◇ A
                    ♣ 7 4
```

The secret is not to cover the first of two honours in sequence. If East withholds the king of spades when the queen is played, the contract will be bound to fail.

Now try this deal:

```
                    ♠ 5
                    ♡ Q 8 6
                    ◇ Q J 10 9
                    ♣ K Q 8 5 3
```

```
                    ♠ Q J 7 4
                    ♡ A K J 5
                    ◇ K 7 4
                    ♣ A 4
```

Against three no-trumps the lead is the six of spades and East goes up with the ace and returns the ten. Now play on.

Automatic to cover the ten of spades with either your queen or jack, wasn't it? Well, if you did, and West is alert and ducks this trick to you, you are down. East turns out to have the ace of diamonds and plays his third spade through your remaining spades and the defence now has four tricks in spades and their ace of diamonds. You forgot your hold-up play in favour of covering an honour with an honour. Q-J-x-x when the ace or king goes up on your right constitutes a single stop and with only five cards between your hand and dummy, you must duck twice so on the ten of spades just play the seven and split your honours on the third round. This is another 'Rule of Seven' hand. The ♠ Q-J constitute your one stop and must not be committed too early. You will see from the full deal that the defence is now powerless.

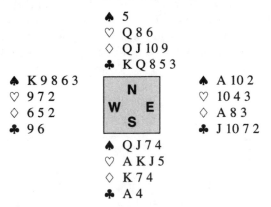

```
                    ♠ 5
                    ♡ Q 8 6
                    ◇ Q J 10 9
                    ♣ K Q 8 5 3
  ♠ K 9 8 6 3         N          ♠ A 10 2
  ♡ 9 7 2                        ♡ 10 4 3
  ◇ 6 5 2          W     E       ◇ A 8 3
  ♣ 9 6               S          ♣ J 10 7 2
                    ♠ Q J 7 4
                    ♡ A K J 5
                    ◇ K 7 4
                    ♣ A 4
```

East could try the good play of the ten of spades at trick one, but declarer can still get home by refusing to win the trick.

Timing

This simply means the order in which a player tackles his suits and is of vital importance on many hands. On the deal below you have become declarer in three no-trumps and received the lead of the queen of hearts.

```
                    ♠ A J 6 4 2
                    ♡ 8 2
                    ◇ K 5
                    ♣ A J 6 3
```

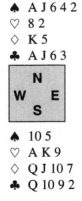

```
                    ♠ 10 5
                    ♡ A K 9
                    ◇ Q J 10 7
                    ♣ Q 10 9 2
```

The Rule of Seven says, duck, so you do and win the continuation with the king of hearts. Now did you run the queen of clubs? If you did you went down because East had the king and cleared the hearts and West had the ace of diamonds which you couldn't avoid letting him win to cash his remaining hearts. A count of top tricks would tell you that you needed at least one diamond trick even if the club finesse was right and if it was wrong you needed two. So at trick two play a diamond to dummy's king and if it holds a second diamond back to hand. If this also wins you play a third diamond. If West wins and plays a heart you are now in position to take the club finesse and not mind if it loses. Look at the full deal.

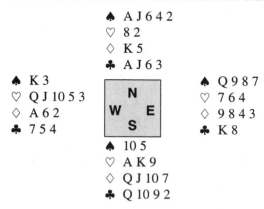

```
                    ♠ A J 6 4 2
                    ♡ 8 2
                    ◇ K 5
                    ♣ A J 6 3
  ♠ K 3                              ♠ Q 9 8 7
  ♡ Q J 10 5 3      N                ♡ 7 6 4
  ◇ A 6 2       W       E            ◇ 9 8 4 3
  ♣ 7 5 4           S                ♣ K 8
                    ♠ 10 5
                    ♡ A K 9
                    ◇ Q J 10 7
                    ♣ Q 10 9 2
```

The way to decide whether to knock out an opponent's ace before attempting to finesse, or vice versa, is dictated by the principle 'attack the entry or possible entry in the danger hand first'. If West, the danger hand, held the king of clubs it was never an entry for him, but the ace of diamonds was, so that suit had to be tackled first. Now move the five-card heart suit into East's hand, giving West two small black cards and the three-card heart holding. This time the lead is the nine of hearts, clearly a short suit lead. Again you duck and win at trick two. But this time you run the queen of clubs next. Why? Well, if East has the king of clubs, you must make him take it early while you still have a heart stop. If he has ace of diamonds as well, then the contract was doomed from the outset, no matter how skilled declarer was. However, if you are lucky and the two key cards are divided, when West wins with ace of diamonds after three rounds of hearts have gone he cannot put East back in for his winning hearts.

Ensuring a Second Stop

♠ J 4
♡ Q 10 8
◇ K 7 4
♣ Q J 10 9 2

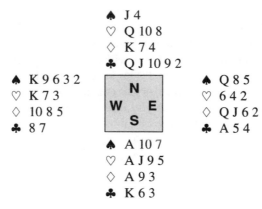

♠ A 10 7
♡ A J 9 5
◇ A 9 3
♣ K 6 3

Try to work this one out yourselves from the above clue!

A low spade is led at trick one to this three no-trump contract. Play it out before you look at the full deal.

Did you put on the jack of spades at trick 1, with the idea that if West has led away from both the king and queen the jack will win? Well, that would be right were it not for the happy chance that in your own hand along with the ace of spades, the certain stopper, is the ten. Now there is no need to commit the jack. Just play low from dummy and if East has neither the king nor queen of spades it is the ten that will win the second spade trick for you. However, East plays the queen of spades on the four. Do you cover with the ace or hold up? Have a look at the full deal now that you know how the spades lie.

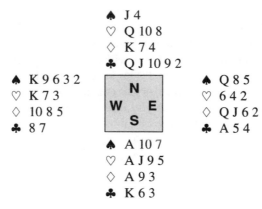

♠ J 4
♡ Q 10 8
◇ K 7 4
♣ Q J 10 9 2

♠ K 9 6 3 2
♡ K 7 3
◇ 10 8 5
♣ 8 7

♠ Q 8 5
♡ 6 4 2
◇ Q J 6 2
♣ A 5 4

♠ A 10 7
♡ A J 9 5
◇ A 9 3
♣ K 6 3

Well, if you ducked the queen of spades you would be defeated. This is not a time for the Rule of Seven. Simply kill the queen of spades with the ace and attack clubs. When the defence carry on with their spades, the jack of spades in dummy faces the guarded ten in your own hand, and you must score a second trick in the suit and make your contract.

Unblocking

You learnt about unblocking in its simplest form as a novice. It simply meant cashing the high cards at the top of the shorter holding leaving yourself in the long holding and able to run off the rest of the suit. Now we need to show you a couple of examples of unblocking allied to creating an entry to the unblocked suit. Look at this deal. As always you are in three no-trumps and West has led the ten of spades.

♠ Q J
♡ 8 7 6
♢ K Q J 8 7 4
♣ 8 3

♠ A K 2
♡ A 5 3 2
♢ A
♣ K J 6 4 2

Did you handle things so that you were able to get to dummy to enjoy that lovely diamond suit? If you did then you really worked out the whole hand at trick one – and we hope that you will do just that every time you sit down at the bridge table. It is vitally important to overtake with the ace or king of spades at trick one, so that you can get rid of the blocking ace of diamonds and get back to dummy to cash the rest of the suit by leading your two of spades to your queen on table. In fact, that little two of spades is a vitally important card and if you squander it on the first trick you've lost your communication with dummy and any defence will mop you up in no time at all.

There's no need to show you the whole deal here. The defence can do nothing to beat you – only you yourself can do that. Let's move on to the next one.

You are playing three no-trumps and West leads the jack of spades.

♠ K Q 3 2
♡ K 3
◇ A K 9 8 2
♣ 8 6

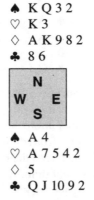

♠ A 4
♡ A 7 5 4 2
◇ 5
♣ Q J 10 9 2

Nice-looking contract, isn't it? Seven top tricks, a double stop in every suit (three in the enemy suit!) and the clubs will easily produce three more tricks. So naturally you unblocked the spade suit by letting the jack of spades run round to your ace and then you led a club. All will be well if the defence hops nimbly up with a top club and you win whatever is played next and return to the club suit which can now be established with the ace of hearts as an entry. But did you consider what might go wrong if the defenders had learned a bit about ducking and allowed you to win the first round of clubs of clubs and only took one of their stoppers in the suit on the second round? Do you think it wouldn't make any difference? Well, study the full deal below and you will see that you misplayed the hand at trick one.

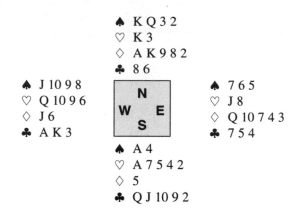

♠ K Q 3 2
♡ K 3
◇ A K 9 8 2
♣ 8 6

♠ J 10 9 8
♡ Q 10 9 6
◇ J 6
♣ A K 3

♠ 7 6 5
♡ J 8
◇ Q 10 7 4 3
♣ 7 5 4

♠ A 4
♡ A 7 5 4 2
◇ 5
♣ Q J 10 9 2

The ace of spades is a vital entry in your hand so that when you get the clubs established you can get back to enjoy them. It is very short-sighted to use it at trick one. Forget about unblocking spades. Win with the king of spades at trick one and start clubs from dummy. Now, however the defence plays, and even if their clubs had been distributed differently, you have the two vital entries to your hand and dummy's ace of diamonds will let you back to table to take the last spade trick.

In fact, this hand was an exercise not in unblocking but in detecting that there was no need so to do. It was really an entry- preserving exercise!

34
Safety Plays

'Safety Play' is a term used in bridge to describe the way declarer should play a certain combination of cards in one suit to make sure a bad break of the missing cards doesn't cost him more tricks than he can afford to lose. You will certainly know by now that if you are missing six cards in a suit, they are mathematically more likely to break 4-2 than 3-3. If there are five cards missing they will break 3-2 more than twice as often as they break 4-1.

To make a safety play means to guard against an unusually bad distribution in the trump suit or a side suit which could break an otherwise sound contract. These tactics are an absolute 'must' in rubber bridge where the primary object is always to make your contract. The same applies to the teams events played in duplicate, where the scoring is by International Match Points.

Playing duplicate pairs scored by match points it is rarely correct to make a safety play, the essence of which is to give up one or more tricks that you could make if the cards lie favourably, in favour of making your contract. In duplicate pairs it is often not enough just to make your contract – overtricks are of supreme importance. If you go against the odds when the rest of the pairs holding your cards don't, and there was no need for you to make a safety play, you will score just as badly for failing to make an overtrick as you would have for going down in your contract. The exception to this is when you find yourself in a contact that you do not expect to be reached at other tables. Then it may be correct to play safe. Remember, playing rubber-bridge, never risk your contract for the sake of an overtrick – look for a safety play.

The hand below is a classic example of what we have been saying:

♠ A 9 8 2
♡ A 6 5
◇ 5 2
♣ K Q 5 2

```
    N
  W   E
    S
```

♠ K 10 7 5 3
♡ K Q 9 8
◇ A K
♣ A 7

Put yourself in the South seat as declarer in six spades. You can see that if the trumps break 2-2 (40.7% of the time) you will make all thirteen tricks. If they break 3-1 (49.7% of the time) you will lose one trump trick however they lie, and make your contract. The only risk to your contract, then, is a 4-0 break, and though this is only a 9.6% chance, you can afford to allow for it. The certain way to make the contract, even if the worst befalls, is to win whatever is led – let's say it's the queen of diamonds – and to lead the three of spades, just covering whatever card West plays. This means that you will play dummy's nine of spades unless West's card is one of the missing honours when you will play the ace of spades.

If West holds all four of the missing cards the nine of spades will win, and you will still lose only the one trump trick you were allowing for. If West shows out when you play the three of spades you know that East has all four missing ones. You simply go up with the ace and finesse against the marked ♠ Q-J on the way back. Had you happened to win the first trick in dummy, your play would have been exactly the same, as you would have returned the two of spades towards your own hand, just covering whatever East plays, and again only losing one trump trick however the missing cards are divided. The important point to understand here is that, in making a play which will ensure your contract however the cards lie, you give up the chance of an overtrick if they do happen to break 2-2 or 3-1 with a singleton honour.

Another way to make a safety play is to refuse a finesse which has a 50% chance of succeeding, because you can ensure your contract another way. You will give up the chance of an overtrick, slender as the risk may seem, against the possibility going down. On the following hand, the risk is very high.

♠ Q 8 7 3
♡ 6 4 3
◇ A K 3
♣ A 7 2

♠ A J 10 4 2
♡ A K 5
◇ 6 4 2
♣ K 9

You are South, declarer in four spades against which West leads the jack of diamonds. You put on dummy's king and East drops the queen. Maybe the queen of diamonds is just an unblocking card but maybe it isn't! You're missing seven diamonds and although a 5-2 break is more likely than 6-1, why risk it when you need only ten tricks for your contract? You can afford the safety play of refusing the trump finesse in favour of playing ace and another spade straight away. If the king of spades is with East (only a 50% chance) then you have given up an overtrick, but if you finesse and West has king of spades and East has any two trumps and that queen of diamonds of his was a singleton, then you may well go down.

Here's another hand on which you, sitting South as declarer in three no-trumps, should choose a safety play.

♠ 8 4 3
♡ 7 5 2
◇ A K Q 7 4 3
♣ J

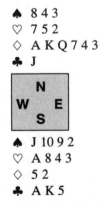

♠ J 10 9 2
♡ A 8 4 3
◇ 5 2
♣ A K 5

West leads a low club and dummy's jack holds. The right play now is a low diamond from dummy. You need only five diamond tricks for your game and the suit will break 4-1 against you 28% of the time. The low diamond will guard against this, as, with all suits held, you will still be able to get back to dummy to take your five diamond tricks. It goes without saying that had you received a heart lead you couldn't have afforded the safety play and would have needed the diamonds to break 3-2. So don't penalise partner for his imaginative leap to three no-trumps over your opening one no-trump. On this deal, even playing duplicate pairs it would be reasonable to use the safety play as many of the pairs won't be in game, so making the contract is always going to be a good score for you.

There are numerous safety plays to be made in the ways of tackling certain combinations of cards so as to produce a guaranteed minimum number of tricks, and if you want to become a really good player you will have to learn the most common of them. Here's a hand that illustrates two of the most common combinations in one deal:

You are South playing in four spades after East dealt and opened the bidding with one diamond.

♠ A 9 7 6
♡ A 4 3
◇ K 2
♣ K 8 7 5

♠ K Q 10 8 5
♡ K Q 10 8 5
◇ 9
♣ 3 2

West leads a low diamond to the queen and you ruff the return of the ace of diamonds. The bidding marks East with the ace of clubs so you must allow for two club losers. This, however, needn't bother you as long as you can bring in both major suits without loss. Can anything go wrong so that you could lose a trump trick? Yes, if all four missing trumps are in one hand. If this should be so, you can pick them up by *leading the king of spades first*. A careless lead of low to the ace will cost you the contract, as when you see East is void you won't be able to do anything about it. Provided you lead the king of spades first, it doesn't matter who holds the jack of spades, as you will be able to pick it up with a finesse.

Trumps having been safely gathered in, turn your attention to the heart suit. This time there are five cards in the opposing hands including the ♡ J-9-8. If the five break 3-2 it won't matter how you play. However, if they break 4-1 and the singleton is not the jack, you can only pick them up if East has the four-card holding. In other words, if West has four to the jack there's nothing you can do about it and your contract is doomed. So once again you cross your fingers and pray that the cards lie as you want them to do. But don't rely on the 3-2 break when you *can* cater for four in the East hand. Cash the king of hearts first and then lead low towards the ace, finessing against the jack of hearts on the way back if West shows out. Note that it's not the same at all if you play low to the ace of hearts on the first round of hearts. If everyone follows, what do you do next? You don't know whether to finesse for the jack of hearts or play for the drop because you won't have seen West's play to the second heart trick.

These are the types of hands on which, given normal breaks of the missing cards in the suits concerned, every declarer will make his contract, whether he knows about safety plays or not. The good player will automatically handle the suits correctly, and will make his contract on the occasions when the cards lie badly for him. This is what safety plays – and this chapter – are all about. So don't rely on being lucky, learn your common safety plays, and you will never have to say to partner 'sorry, nothing I could do about it – how could I know the cards were going to break so badly?'

We have only outlined the basic technique of safety plays, and hope you will see that the correct handling of the cards is largely a matter of common sense and deduction. Sometimes you'll be able to cope with a bad break in any of the opposing hands. Sometimes your cards will be such that you can cope only with a bad break in one of the opposing hands, not the other. Play to give yourself that chance. As Terence Reese says in his book on safety plays, it is not necessary to count the hands or know the adverse distribution: all you need to realise is that a particular suit may break badly. It is enough when you are playing a contract that seems to be lay-down, to pause and say to yourself: 'Can I lose this contract if the breaks are extremely bad?' If the answer is yes, then look for a safety play that will protect you against such distribution. Pretty well always you will find that if you have two top honours in one hand facing one in the other, you can initiate the safety play by cashing one of the two top honours first.

Table of Percentage Plays

Dummy & Declarer hold	Number Missing	Possible Distributions	Percentage of Frequency
In any one suit: 4 cards	9	5-4	58.9%
		6-3	31.4%
		7-2	8.6%
		8-1	1.1%
		9-0	0.0%
5 cards	8	5-3	47.1%
		4-4	32.7%
		6-2	17.1%
		7-1	2.9%
		8-0	0.2%
6 cards	7	4-3	62.2%
		5-2	30.5%
		6-1	6.8%
		7-0	0.5%
7 cards	6	4-2	48.4%
		3-3	35.5%
		5-1	14.5%
		6-0	1.5%
8 cards	5	3-2	67.8%
		4-1	28.3%
		5-0	3.9%
9 cards	4	3-1	49.7%
		2-2	40.7%
		4-0	9.6%
10 cards	3	2-1	78.0%
		3-0	22.0%
11 cards	2	1-1	52.0%
		2-0	48.0%

PART III
DEFENCE

25
Choosing the Opening Lead

The most difficult thing about opening leads is choosing the suit in which to attack. Once you have decided on that, knowing which card to lead from any particular holding is a matter of learning as much as you can of the Table of Standard Leads, set out on later. We give below the general principles for selecting your lead, but they are only guidelines and as you become more experienced you will realise that there are always exceptions to all of them.

Blind Leads Against Suit Contracts

1 **Don't:** lead away from a tenace (a broken honour sequence).

2 **Don't:** underlead an ace or away from a single unsupported honour card – however, this is sometimes unavoidable against a low-level contract.

3 **Do:** lead the ace from the ace-king of an unbid suit. This is an excellent lead because it almost invariably leaves you on lead to trick two after you have seen dummy and your partner's signal.

4 **Do:** lead the top of a sequence (three cards), near sequence or interior sequence.

5 **Don't:** lead a short suit to get a ruff if you have trump length, or a holding like K-x in trumps.

6 **Do:** consider leading a trump, unless you have four or a singleton.

Blind Leads Against No-Trump Contracts

1 **Don't:** automatically lead your own long suit when you have a bad hand with no outside entry.

2 **Don't:** lead your own suit when it has been bid by declarer or dummy unless you are sure your holding is strong enough for this to be constructive.

3   **Do:** attack in any five-card suit that you have a clear hope of establishing.

4   **Do:** lead tops of sequences or near sequences, not an automatic 'fourth best'.

5   **Do:** lead your shortest suit (top of nothing) if you do not want to lead your longest, perhaps because it is a poor four-card holding headed by an isolated honour. The idea is that this might well be partner's best suit and the one he would have led had he been on lead.

Leading Partner's Bid Suit

You need a very good reason for not attacking in the suit bid by your partner, particularly if he has overcalled. One reason might be that you have only a singleton of his suit and a good suit of your own that looks as if it might become established. If you lead partner's suit – and this turns out badly – you will at least win the post-mortem! Selecting which card differs slightly as to whether you are defending a no-trump contract or a suit contract.

Against a no-trump contract: lead low away from three or more cards to an honour, top of nothing and the top of three cards headed by two honours, e.g. Q-J-8.

Against a trump contract, consider leading the top card of your partner's suit, especially when you have actually supported his bid during the auction.

MUD Leads

Short-suit leads in trump contracts are made for two reasons. The first, of course, is in the hope of getting a ruff, the other being when it seems the safest thing to do to safeguard your other assets. When your worthless holding is a trebleton – and partner plays you for a doubleton – the defence may lose the tempo trying to get the ruff. For this reason many partnerships lead top of any doubleton and the middle card from a trebleton, and follow it on the next round with the up card, and, obviously, on the third round the lowest card, hence the MUD standing for Middle, Up, Down.

A 'top of nothing' holding really is three worthless cards and never headed by an honour, even the ten. You've got to throw the 'up' card on the second round of the suit, and could well give away a trick this way. Never make a MUD lead in a suit bid by your partner and leave MUD leads in no-trumps for the experts as they can so easily cause confusion when partner is trying to apply the Rule of Eleven.

This lead style does have many advantages but before you adopt it, consider its disadvantages, too! Declarer reads your card holding also, and knows whether he has to ruff high, or not at all, because dummy's card will win the third round of the suit. Partner very often knows from the bidding whether your lead was a doubleton or trebleton but declarer is less likely to know the exact distribution of the enemy hands.

It's terribly important to listen to the way your opponents bid on the way to the final contract. (We don't mean remembering that partner bid and what he bid, because then you have, more often than not, an obvious suit to lead!). This is often why the less bidding you do on the way to your contract, the less likely you are to help your opponents to find the killing lead. If the bidding against you has gone 1NT – 3NT, you have little idea who holds what, other than the fact that dummy is unlikely to hold a major suit, and whereas opener's hand was limited, responder's was not. He has anything from about 13 to 18 points. Look at your own cards and try to picture how many points your partner could hold. Your opponents have (working on a known 12–14 points for the opening no-trump) between 25 and 32, so if you hold, say, 8 points, partner can't have more than 7 points at best, and might have only 1 or 2. If your hand is a complete bust though, you can visualise partner with some points, up to 14 anyway. Suppose you are on lead after this auction.

North	South
1◇	1♠
2♠	2NT
3NT	

North-South stretched to reach the game contract, so you know partner must have some values, and the less you have, the more you can picture with him. Now let's look at some hands for you, playing West, to hold and to lead from against the auction shown::

West		North	South
♠ 7 5 3		Pass	1♠
♡ 9 7 2		1NT	2◇
◇ A J 10 2		2♠	Pass
♣ K Q J			

You might well think that the 'obvious lead' was the king of clubs, but think again. The bidding has given you the clue. South is two-suited in spades and diamonds, and North has given preference to spades whilst you have good diamonds. Attack the trumps before South can ruff out the diamonds. If you don't, your good diamonds will fall under North's trumps for sure. You may not defeat two spades, but there isn't a better line to try.

West	North	South
♠ J 8 7 5	1◇	1♠
♡ 8 4 3	3◇	3NT
◇ J 4 3		
♣ A 9 6		

Defending a no-trump contract this time, clearly you can't lead a spade because of South's bid on your right. What about the eight of hearts, the top-of-nothing? Or perhaps the six of clubs, though you discarded this on the grounds that partner might think it was a fourth best. What about the ace of clubs? You must make an attacking lead if you are going to defeat this contract, as South probably has six diamonds to cash as soon as he wins a trick, and may well have bid no-trumps with clubs or hearts wide open, rather like a 'gambling' three no-trump opening bid. Make the only lead that allows you to take a look at dummy and see what partner signals..

West	North	South
♠ 6 4	1♡	1NT
♡ K Q 8 4		
◇ A J 6 3 2		
♣ 8 6		

Clearly partner has points, as the bidding has died so quickly. There is no reason to do anything other than lead the 'obvious' three of diamonds.

West	North	South
♠ K 6	1♠	3◇
♡ 9 3 6	3♠	4NT
◇ J 6 4 2	5♡	5NT
♣ 8 7 6 3	6◇	7NT

Listening carefully to the auction here you know that North has at least five spades, two aces and a king and that South, having shown a strong hand by his three diamond bid, is quite happy about the ace-king position for the grand slam. But you know two things he doesn't! You know that North's king isn't in spades, and also that diamonds are breaking badly for declarer. Now what about your lead?

How about the six of spades? Are you horrified? Yes, of course you are! You have remembered that we say never lead away from an unsupported honour, but it's a bit different when you're leading against a freely bid grand slam. Put yourself in South's seat. Here he is at trick one faced with a choice of whether or not to finesse spades for his grand slam! If he can see any other way to make his contract, he'll refuse the finesse and then, when he finds that the diamonds aren't working, it will be too late for him to wish he'd played differently. If you let him find out (around trick 8 or so) that he has no other play for his contract than to finesse for king of spades, then finesse he will, so make life difficult for him. That's what you're there for as a defender, you know.

West		North	South
♠ K 2		–	1♠
♡ A 7 4 2		2♡	3♡
◇ 5 4 3 2		4♠	4NT
♣ A 6 3		5♣	5♠

If you've been listening carefully here you'll be in no doubt as to exactly what to lead. The ace of hearts it has to be. Why? Well, North has shown a nice major two-suiter by this delayed game raise sequence and South was interested enough to try for a slam, but gave up when he found that North had no aces. Don't just sit back and wait to cash your two aces and your trump trick. If you lead a passive diamond, you might get a nasty shock if North happened to be void in clubs.

Now where's the defence's third trick coming from? You know partner has at most one heart in his hand, so if he has even one trump you can give him a ruff at trick two. Be careful to lead the two of hearts at trick two for him to ruff – as long, of course, as there's a club in dummy. This suit preference signal is fully explained in the next chapter. Thus you direct him to put you back on lead with a club to give him a second ruff, and now the contract goes three down. If you happen to be playing duplicate pairs, this defence will almost certainly give you a 'top'.

Now we'll look at two hands where you have to find an opening lead after either you or your partner has bid during the auction. The first example is what we call a mandatory lead.

West	West	North	East	South
♠ A K 10 6	–	Pass	Pass	1♡
♡ 2	Double	All Pass		
◇ Q J 10 8				
♣ K Q 8 5				

Take your fingers off the ace of spades and put them on the two of hearts! Why? Because by passing your take-out double, your partner has said he holds the hearts – something like ♡ Q-J-10-8-7 and a bit outside, and you must ensure that declarer can't get any joy out of the one or two little trumps that dummy may hold. Don't forget this one – when partner makes a 'free' pass of your take-out double, your only alibi for not leading a trump is that you haven't got one!

West	West	North	East	South
♠ 10 9 8 7	–	–	–	1NT
♡ K 8 5	Pass	3NT	Double	All Pass
◇ 9 7 6 2				
♣ 9 3				

This lead is not so much mandatory as conventional. Had partner not doubled you would have led the sensible ten of spades, but he has doubled a freely bid three no-trumps, perhaps at some risk. He is saying that he wants you to lead your shortest suit, in this case clubs. He probably holds something like:

♠ A 4
♡ 7 4 2
◇ 8 3
♣ K Q J 10 8 4

So he's pretty sure you will hold less clubs than any other suit and, therefore, if he leaves you alone to make your own choice, the club is the last thing you'll pick on. In fact, your 'obvious' ten of spades will knock out his only entry, and he'll never be able to get in to enjoy his clubs.

This is by no means the only way to play this type of double. We have seen it used in three other ways; firstly to ask specifically for the defender on lead to start with a spade, secondly their shortest major, or finally a heart.

26
Signalling

The opening lead is made, dummy goes down on the table and declarer starts to try to make his contract. Maybe he simply cannot be defeated but the defenders must keep trying to the bitter end, particularly if playing duplicate where stopping overtricks can score as well as bidding and making a grand slam!

So the defence needs every weapon it can find and communication between the partners is absolutely essential. In an expert game every card played conveys a message. A player can send signals by the card he leads, by the card with which he follows suit to his partner's or declarer's lead, and by the way he discards.

High to Encourage, Low to Discourage

There are many signalling systems but the simplest, and still one of the most effective, is to play 'attitude' signals. The higher the card a player contributes the more interest he shows in that suit, and the lower the card he plays the more he denies any interest or any effective values in the suit. Any card followed by a lower one of the same suit constitutes a peter and shows enthusiasm, while no matter how high a card you play, if you follow it with a higher still one on the next round you are discouraging not encouraging.

It is also possible to show partner the number of cards you hold in a suit by petering to show an even number and by playing the lowest card you hold to show an odd number. This, of course, helps your partner to work out just how many of a given suit are in the hidden hand.

Peter in the Trump Suit

When a player peters in the trump suit, he is saying exactly the opposite to the above. This peter shows more than a doubleton, and an urgent wish to ruff something with this third trump if given the chance. It is particularly valuable when you have led a singleton of another suit, which declarer has won and started to draw trumps and then decided he cannot afford to play a third round. If your partner gets in he knows not only that your lead was a singleton but that you still have a trump left. Failure to peter in trumps, of course, shows you only held a doubleton to begin with.

Discarding

Your partner will watch for your first discard with keen interest as it may be your first opportunity to tell him where your values lie. If you can spare it, discard a high card of the suit you would like him to lead. If you cannot spare a high card of the suit you really want, because you feel it may be a trick-taking card (and this is true particularly when defending a no-trump contract), discard low cards of the suits you don't want. After all, if partner has led clubs and you have contributed the two of clubs and then on the heart suit you eventually discard a low spade, partner can work out that if you have anything at all it will be in the diamond suit.

Suit Preference Signals

When following suit to his partner's lead the first card a defender contributes shows his 'attitude' to that suit, i.e. 'yes, I like it, no, I don't'. If your partner continues with the suit regardless of discouragement from you, then the second card you contribute may give a message about a holding in another suit. This would be a suit preference signal, also known as a Lavinthal or McKenney signal. The 'attitude' signal comes first so it is only occasionally possible to make a suit preference signal at trick one, but it can be done when it is clear that a switch may be coming at trick two – when dummy holds a singleton of the suit led, for example. These signals can sometimes be given by the rank of a card led, too, especially when leading for partner to ruff.

Practised partnerships use these signals when defending no-trump contracts, too, but they are easiest read when defending trump contracts. Disregard the suit on which the message is being given, disregard the trump suit (until you are expert in these signals!) and there remain two suits, one of which is higher ranked than the other. If you want to draw partner's attention to the higher of these 'outside' suits, follow with as high a card as you can spare – an unnecessarily high card. Conversely, if it is the lower-ranking of the other two suits you want to tell partner about, contribute the lowest card you hold.

As always, examples will help!

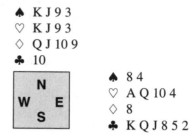

```
        ♠ K J 9 3
        ♡ K J 9 3
        ◇ Q J 10 9
        ♣ 10
                        ♠ 8 4
                        ♡ A Q 10 4
                        ◇ 8
                        ♣ K Q J 8 5 2
```

Defending South's five diamond contract West leads the ace of clubs in response to your opening bid of one club. Two things are clear, first that the ace of clubs will hold the trick, and second that West must switch from clubs at trick two. How is he to decide whether to lead a spade or a heart? Left to himself he can only guess, but you can tell him. Diamonds are trumps and clubs are being played, which leaves spades and hearts. It is vital that West should switch to a heart, so play the two of clubs. This will draw his attention to the hearts, the lower-ranking of the two remaining suits, and he will switch to a heart. Don't confuse this with merely telling him not to continue with clubs – that would be the message if dummy had several little clubs – but here the need for a switch is obvious because of dummy's singleton ten of clubs. Mentally exchange the hearts and spades in your hand, and now you would want a spade lead. Drop the king of clubs on partner's ace. This is an unusually high card, directing his attention to your need for a switch to the higher-ranking of the two remaining suits.

You are West, defending a contract of three spades after the bidding has gone 1♠ – 3♠.

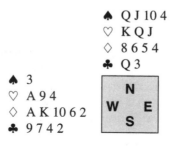

```
                ♠ Q J 10 4
                ♡ K Q J
                ◇ 8 6 5 4
                ♣ Q 3
    ♠ 3
    ♡ A 9 4
    ◇ A K 10 6 2
    ♣ 9 7 4 2
```

You lead the ace of diamonds on which East discards a club so you plan to cash the king of diamonds and lead a third diamond for him to ruff. Now, with your ace of hearts there will be four defensive tricks. Can the defence defeat the contract? Yes, if after East takes his diamond ruff, he returns a heart, not a club. You direct him to do this by leading your highest available diamond, the ten of diamonds, for him to ruff. So next he will return a heart to your ace and you will lead another diamond, giving him his second ruff.

Had you held the ace of clubs instead of the ace of hearts, you would have directed him to return the lower of the two remaining suits (hearts and clubs) by leading your lowest diamond, the two, at trick three. Without the signal East might have returned a heart for the same result, but this would have been a pure guess instead of a certainty. If you hadn't held the ace of hearts, then you would have given him his ruff by leading the six of diamonds, and he would have been hard put to read a message into that! Negative messages such as this can be as important as positive ones.

If a suit has been bid, it is often possible to get across a vital message even when the situation is not absolutely clear cut. This time you are West defending South's six hearts, after East opened with a pre-emptive three diamonds.

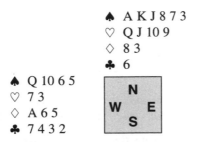

> ♠ A K J 8 7 3
> ♡ Q J 10 9
> ◇ 8 3
> ♣ 6

♠ Q 10 6 5
♡ 7 3
◇ A 6 5
♣ 7 4 3 2

You lead the ace of diamonds though you can't think you're going to get more than one diamond trick, and that won't defeat six hearts. But, surprise, surprise! East drops the queen of diamonds! This can't be a singleton after his three diamond opening, so it must be a signal – a scream for a switch to spades. Lo and behold, when you follow instructions and lead a spade, East turns out to have a void in the suit and gets a ruff to defeat the slam.

Yes, suit preference signals are marvellous, but a word of warning here! They can only be given when the natural message of the card played is unnecessary or has already been sent. If you hold ♡ A-K-Q and lead one against declarer's spade contract and partner follows with the two of hearts, don't for heaven's sake automatically switch to clubs and go to bed with two heart tricks. At present partner only wants to warn you that he cannot help with hearts by producing the queen of hearts or ruffing the third round. Play another round of hearts and look for his second card – that will tell you about the outside suits.

You will also realise that it is easier to ask for the higher outside suit than the lower, as a low card can also mean lack of interest in anything! Just note that partner certainly does not want the higher suit or he could have tried to say so.

Dropping the Queen

You already know, when leading a side suit against a trump contract, holding the ace-king you lead the ace, and that, therefore, to show the ace-king bare you lead the king first and follow with the ace.

When your partner leads the ace of a suit, you confidently expect him to have the king behind it. When petering to encourage the continuation of a suit you must never play the queen from, say, queen-doubleton, but it is correct to peter with the knave from knave-doubleton. You can, therefore, use the play of the queen to convey a special message, and that is that you have both queen and knave. So when partner leads an ace and you find yourself with quene-jack doubleton, if you play the knave, partner will continue with the king and your queen will drop, thus wasting your valuable honour and possibly even making the ten good for declarer. So you play your queen first, which will assure partner that your queen is either singleton or queen-jack doubleton. In either case it will be perfectly safe for partner to lead low at trick two, for you either to ruff or win with the knave.

You aren't confined solely to using this convention when you have no better than a doubleton – suppose you had Q-J-10-9. Your correct play then would be the queen on the opening lead of the ace and, if partner next leads low, play the nine. He will then know your precise holding.

This is a very useful little convention as, according to the situation, it can conserve the partnership's control of a suit or open up the way for a quick ruff. It can also help to preserve communications between defenders' hands, by, for example, allowing the opening leader's partner to win trick two and get in a perhaps vital switch, when declarer would have been ruffing the third round of the suit.

Ace Lead Against a No-Trump Contract

As stated above, the standard lead from a suit headed by an ace-king is the ace, but this is not the case when you are defending a no-trump contract. The usual lead would be fourth highest, or top of nothing. Against a normally-bid no-trump contract, and when the lead is not in a suit bid by partner, the lead of the ace requests partner to play his highest card in the suit.

This request to play the highest available card in the suit has a double purpose, firstly to unblock it, and secondly to clarify for the opening leader the position of the other cards in the suit. Suppose, for example, you find yourself on lead against a no-trump contract and hold a suit such as ♡ A-K-J-10-8-4.

With three honours you always lead one of them, and here the normal choice – had you been playing against a suit contract – would be the ace. If you lead the ace against a no-trump contract your partner should know that he is expected to play his highest card in the suit, so if you didn't want him to do this, perhaps because you held ♡ A-K-8-6-3, you would lead the fourth best, or from ♡ A-K-Q-7-5, the king.

Don't say you couldn't possibly have a suit like this if your opponents had bid correctly. In these days of the weak no-trump it is not at all unknown for both declarer and dummy to be virtually missing one suit. Let's take a quick look at the value of this convention. Assuming that, not using the convention, you lead the 'normal' ace from A-K-J-10-8-4, partner, with three to the queen, will not think to unblock. Nothing helpful having appeared in dummy you won't have any idea of whether to continue the suit – you're not likely to have an outside entry – or whether to try to get partner in to lead through declarer's queen. If partner can be relied on to play his highest card, if it's the queen the suit will be unblocked and you will be able to run off your suit without hindrance. If it's not the queen, you may learn a great deal. For instance, suppose partner drops the seven. Now you know for certain that declarer has the Q-9-6 and that cashing your king and playing a third round won't be any help to you if you have no entry. The convention can also at times reveal a singleton in partner's hand. If he follows with the three, dummy has the four and declarer plays the two, your partner can't have another one!

Even from a shorter suit such as A-K-J-10, the ace would be the best lead. Partner can safely unblock by dropping the queen, and not risk winning the third round, or the leader can switch, and wait for the lead to come through to him.

Leading Against a 'Gambling' Three No-Trump Opening

You must entirely change your ideas about the correct opening lead when you are up against a three no-trump opening bid. What do you know about declarer's hand? That he has a running minor and virtually nothing outside. So an ordinary fourth best lead, unless you strike very lucky, is hardly likely to be of much help. Lead an ace if you have one, both to see the table, and to try to get a signal from partner as to what you should do next. Partner must, of course, be really 'with it' on signals. He mustn't carelessly follow with the card nearest his thumb when following to your ace, but must try to get across to you where his strength lies. Seeing dummy too may give you a lot of help as to how to continue.

Here's a complete deal to illustrate what we mean:

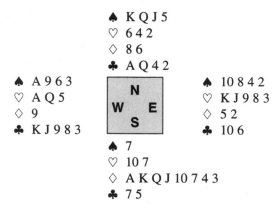

           ♠ K Q J 5
           ♡ 6 4 2
           ◇ 8 6
           ♣ A Q 4 2

♠ A 9 6 3   ♠ 10 8 4 2
♡ A Q 5   ♡ K J 9 8 3
◇ 9   ◇ 5 2
♣ K J 9 8 3   ♣ 10 6

           ♠ 7
           ♡ 10 7
           ◇ A K Q J 10 7 4 3
           ♣ 7 5

West is on lead against South's opening three no-trumps. He knows, of course, that South's suit must be diamonds, but if there is to be any hope of defeating the contract, West must hit on the right line of defence. He must not lead his fourth best club, as he would do in the normal way – as you can see, all that would happen would be that South would go up with dummy's ace of clubs and run his eight diamond tricks. So West should lead the ace of spades, both to take a look at dummy and to see partner's reaction. Well, the sight of dummy's spades makes it clear that there's no hope in that suit, and this is confirmed by East's two of spades. So next West should try the ace of hearts and, Eureka! – the nine comes from East. West cashes the queen of hearts and continues with the five of hearts and the defence takes five heart tricks plus the ace of spades.

27
Defence

Unless you are a very lucky card holder you'll spend at least half your time at the bridge table defending your opponents' contract, the other half of the time being divided between being declarer and being dummy. Defence is more challenging and, we think, just as enjoyable as being declarer. Many points are won, and good scores achieved in duplicate, by defeating the other side as by making your own contracts.

Good defence starts by leading and continues with accurate signalling, both of which aspects are discussed in Chapters 25 and 26. Now we must look at some of the many other tactics which you will need to master.

Switching

One of the pieces of helpful advice freely showered on you is 'always return your partner's suit'. Rubbish! We say, think carefully before you automatically return partner's suit, as very often this is just what declarer is praying you will do when, in fact, what you should have done is switch to another suit before it's too late. Of course there are many occasions when you can't be sure whether a switch is right or not, but you'll be surprised when you study the hands in the following pages how obvious it is if you only think instead of playing automatically.

Here's a nice easy one to start with:

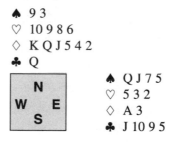

```
            ♠ 9 3
            ♡ 10 9 8 6
            ◇ K Q J 5 4 2
            ♣ Q
        ┌─────────┐      ♠ Q J 7 5
        │    N    │      ♡ 5 3 2
        │  W   E  │      ◇ A 3
        │    S    │      ♣ J 10 9 5
        └─────────┘
```

You are sitting East, defending South's contract of four hearts after the unrevealing bidding sequence 1♡ – 4♡, and your partner leads the ten of diamonds. As both you and declarer study dummy, you feel that partner hasn't exactly chosen the best lead from your point of view. Declarer covers the ten of diamonds with the jack, you play your ace of diamonds and declarer follows with the seven of diamonds. If dummy hadn't held all those trumps you might have tried holding up for one round, but somehow it doesn't look the right thing to do with this hand. If you blindly return the three of diamonds, thinking that there's plenty of time for partner to make some tricks, because the bidding marks him with some points somewhere, you will have presented declarer with an unmakeable contract.

Clearly you must switch, but to what? A trump isn't going to do much and anyway, if your side got a trump trick coming to you, it will come in its own good time. Had you been on lead yourself at trick one you'd probably have decided to lead the jack of clubs, but will that do you any good now? One glance at dummy will tell you that there will be at most one club trick for the defence, so what about spades? Now you've got there. Your hope should be that declarer holds something like ♠ K-x, that you can gather in two spade tricks immediately to add to your ace of diamonds, and that partner holds something like ♡ K-x. So you play your five of spades at trick 2 – or do you? Well, if it's your lucky day partner will hold ♠ A-10 and your error will go unpunished. But the correct card to lead is the queen of spades, in the hope that partner has the ace over declarer's ♠ K-10. Here is the full deal:

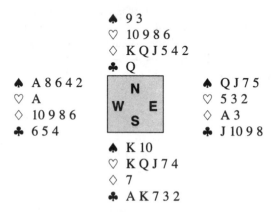

Now aren't you glad you didn't blindly return a diamond at trick 2? If you had, declarer would have had no problems.

Have a look at this next one. This time you are East defending South's contract of three no-trumps, the bidding having gone (with East-West silent) 1♣ – 3♣ – 3NT. West leads the jack of spades. Try to decide for yourself how you would defend.

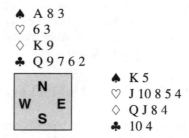

```
            ♠ A 8 3
            ♡ 6 3
            ◇ K 9
            ♣ Q 9 7 6 2
                              ♠ K 5
                              ♡ J 10 8 5 4
                              ◇ Q J 8 4
                              ♣ 10 4
```

Declarer plays the three of spades on West's jack and your king wins. Are you going to return partner's suit? If you rush to do this you are guilty of woolly thinking, or worse still, not thinking at all! You know that declarer holds the queen of spades because the lead has told you so, so there's no future in spades for the defence. Declarer has shown around 16 points by his rebid, and he is bound to hold top clubs. Adding your points and dummy's to 16, you can tell that there's room for West to hold one ace, but not two (there are only 40 points in the pack!). You must play him for heart honours, because if his ace is the ace of diamonds, and South has the top clubs, he will wrap up five clubs, two spades, the ace of hearts and dummy's king of diamonds, if you play a diamond back to partner. Switch to the jack of hearts with fingers crossed that partner holds the ♡ A-Q. If you are right, and the full deal is as shown below, you will sink the contract by two, and if you are wrong, well then, South could always make nine tricks.

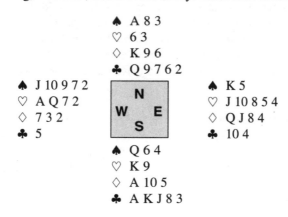

```
                    ♠ A 8 3
                    ♡ 6 3
                    ◇ K 9 6
                    ♣ Q 9 7 6 2
    ♠ J 10 9 7 2                      ♠ K 5
    ♡ A Q 7 2                         ♡ J 10 8 5 4
    ◇ 7 3 2                           ◇ Q J 8 4
    ♣ 5                               ♣ 10 4
                    ♠ Q 6 4
                    ♡ K 9
                    ◇ A 10 5
                    ♣ A K J 8 3
```

Has it crossed your mind to wonder if declarer made a mistake at trick one and that he should have played his ace of spades? Well no, he didn't, because to come to his ninth trick he had counted that he had either to make the king of hearts, which meant finding you with the ace of hearts, or the lead may have been from ♠ K-J-10, so he was right to play low in dummy at trick one. If the cards lay as badly as he feared, his only chance was a less than perfect defence, so he allowed himself the extra hope that you would go wrong at trick two.

Unblocking

Defenders must be careful not to block the run of partner's suit. Here is an example from a no-trump contract. Your partner overcalled the opening bid of one diamond with a weak two hearts, and when North bid three clubs, South tried three no-trumps.

Your partner leads the queen of hearts and this is what you see:

```
        ♠ K J 9
        ♡ 7 6
        ◇ K 2
        ♣ K J 9 8 7 5
```
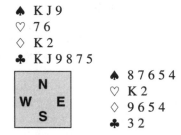
```
                       ♠ 8 7 6 5 4
                       ♡ K 2
                       ◇ 9 6 5 4
                       ♣ 3 2
```

If you happily let partner's queen of hearts hold the first trick you have killed the defence stone dead. Declarer, who clearly holds the ace of hearts, ducks and partner continues with the jack of hearts on which you now put your king of hearts. Declarer lets you hold the trick and now what? You should have overtaken at trick one and let partner win the second round of the suit so that he could continue to drive out declarer's ace – which you cannot do.

Look at the full deal below and see that provided the heart suit is cleared, when declarer starts on clubs your partner takes his ace of clubs at once and cashes his remaining hearts, setting the contract by at least two tricks. If you block his heart suit then declarer cannot fail to make his contract.

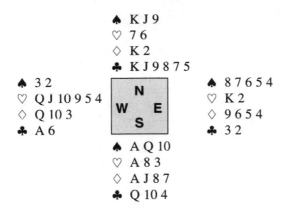

Unblocking is not only essential in the defence of no-trump contracts. It can occur in suit contracts too. This time declarer is playing in Four Hearts, and your partner leads the king of clubs:

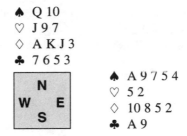

Don't be miserly and just happily play your nine of clubs at trick one, keeping your ace of clubs for the second round. Your partner's lead surely promised at least the queen of clubs and hopefully the jack of clubs or ten. If you duck you block the suit. Overtake and clear the way for partner to take his club tricks, discarding the nine of spades on the third round. Even safer would be to cash your ace of spades before returning the nine of clubs. Look at the full deal below and see that if you block the run of the clubs, declarer will unblock the diamonds and end up in dummy after drawing trumps to take discards on his good diamonds.

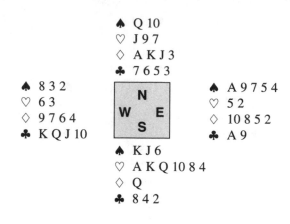

```
              ♠ Q 10
              ♡ J 9 7
              ◇ A K J 3
              ♣ 7 6 5 3
♠ 8 3 2                        ♠ A 9 7 5 4
♡ 6 3          N              ♡ 5 2
◇ 9 7 6 4    W     E          ◇ 10 8 5 2
♣ K Q J 10     S              ♣ A 9
              ♠ K J 6
              ♡ A K Q 10 8 4
              ◇ Q
              ♣ 8 4 2
```

Ducking

Do you remember about ducking a trick early on in a suit when you were declarer and there was no outside entry to this suit? Now you must learn to duck in exactly the same way when you are a defender with no outside entry to your suit. This time you are holding the West cards and the bidding has gone:

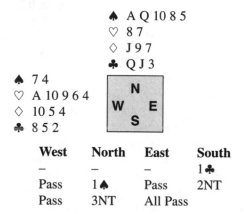

```
              ♠ A Q 10 8 5
              ♡ 8 7
              ◇ J 9 7
              ♣ Q J 3
♠ 7 4
♡ A 10 9 6 4    N
◇ 10 5 4      W     E
♣ 8 5 2         S
```

West	North	East	South
–	–	–	1♣
Pass	1♠	Pass	2NT
Pass	3NT	All Pass	

You make the obvious lead of the six of hearts on which partner plays the king of hearts and declarer follows with the five of hearts. Partner returns the three of hearts covered by declarer with the queen. Do you happily (and thoughtlessly!) slap on the ace and lead another to clear the suit? If you do, you've cooked your goose for sure. Before you automatically cover the queen of hearts, count the suit. You can now see eleven hearts and know that the two missing ones are the jack of hearts and two of hearts. Can your partner hold both? If he does, then declarer has bid like a lunatic and your partner has deliberately deceived you when he returned the three of hearts, as his correct return would have been the two of hearts. Could partner have held ♡ K-J-3 originally? If so he has defended atrociously by not returning the jack of hearts, so you can safely mark declarer with that card, which means that you can't prevent him from winning one heart trick. So choose which one to let him win, and duck now. You are playing for partner to have held ♡ K-3-2 originally and an outside entry, so that when he gets in he can play that vital two of hearts back to you. Now you, the defence, must take four heart tricks plus whatever East gets in with. But what if declarer holds that two of hearts, you will say? Well then, probably the contract was unbeatable anyway, but at least you will have tried the defence most likely to get declarer down if the cards are lying as in the full deal below:

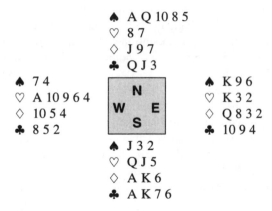

```
                 ♠ A Q 10 8 5
                 ♡ 8 7
                 ◇ J 9 7
                 ♣ Q J 3
  ♠ 7 4                            ♠ K 9 6
  ♡ A 10 9 6 4    N               ♡ K 3 2
  ◇ 10 5 4      W   E             ◇ Q 8 3 2
  ♣ 8 5 2          S               ♣ 10 9 4
                 ♠ J 3 2
                 ♡ Q J 5
                 ◇ A K 6
                 ♣ A K 7 6
```

The vital thing is not to cut communications with your partner. If you were declarer with the West cards as your dummy, and you wanted four tricks in hearts for your contract, you would duck the second heart trick all round, and exactly the same line of play is available to the defence too.

Sometimes it can be just as necessary to duck a trick in the defence to a suit contract to keep communications open between the defenders, often to get in a ruff. This time you are East, defending after a simple sequence where South opened one heart and went on to four hearts over North's raise to three hearts.

♠ 9 8 5
♡ 9 8 6 5
◇ Q 10 3 2
♣ A 5

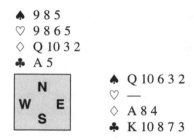

♠ Q 10 6 3 2
♡ —
◇ A 8 4
♣ K 10 8 7 3

West leads the seven of diamonds and, whilst declarer looks at dummy and plans, you, too, must plan. You can see two probable tricks for the defence, the ace of diamonds and the king of clubs, but what about the other two?

What does the lead mean? We hope by now you've done the Rule of Eleven and discovered whether or not it could be a fourth best. Could it? Well, just about, but it's much more likely to be a short-suit lead, so what could it be from? If it's a singleton declarer has five diamonds, and yet he's playing in hearts, never having mentioned diamonds, so it's probably from two or three small cards, either top of nothing or middle of three, according to your lead style. Either way it will cost you nothing to duck. A tricky declarer might try the queen of diamonds, but you should withhold your ace. Your best hope of defeating the contract is that the lead was, the top of a doubleton, and that partner can gain the lead in time to put you back in to give him his ruff, so play the encouraging eight of diamonds at trick one. If the lead were from a three-card holding, then you can't fail to make your ace of diamonds later on, and if South is to be defeated at all, it will have to be by another line of defence. Here's the full deal:

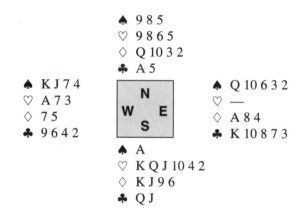

♠ 9 8 5
♡ 9 8 6 5
◇ Q 10 3 2
♣ A 5

♠ K J 7 4
♡ A 7 3
◇ 7 5
♣ 9 6 4 2

♠ Q 10 6 3 2
♡ —
◇ A 8 4
♣ K 10 8 7 3

♠ A
♡ K Q J 10 4 2
◇ K J 9 6
♣ Q J

As the cards lie, when West wins with the ace of hearts, he will lead his five of diamonds to your ace and you will give him his ruff, and your king of clubs is the setting trick. Had his lead been a middle card (MUD) from, say, ◊ 9-7-5, whether you did or didn't duck the diamond would have made no difference, so play for the holding you want in partner's hand, in this case a doubleton. We've already said you must play the eight of diamonds on his seven – if you play the four of diamonds, the last thing he will do when in with the trump ace is continue diamonds! One further point is that if you had held, say, a bare trump ace as well as the ace of diamonds, you would have won the first round of diamonds and returned a diamond, knowing you were bound to win the first round of trumps too. You would have seen whether West's lead was from three or a doubleton, and would have given partner his ruff if it were there. Never give partner a chance to go wrong if you can take charge yourself! The golden rule is duck when you have a reason, not just because you can't bear to part with your high cards! As we've told you already, this is called finessing against partner, a thing you mustn't do without good reason.

You may have noticed that the distribution is such that your side can make four spades, and you might have entered the bidding with the East hand. Still, that is no excuse for letting your opponents make their contract.

28
More About Defence

Now we must take hold-up and ducking plays a stage further. A defender must not always rush to grab his winners in a suit being attacked by declarer, but equally he must not hang on to them so long that he never scores them at all! Accurate signalling between the defenders is essential here.

Rule of the Entryless Dummy

This rule applies when declarer is seeking to establish and run a suit in a dummy that has no outside winners in the other suits. It occurs commonly in no-trump contracts but the same principles apply in a trump contract after trumps have been drawn. Picture yourself sitting East defending South's contract of three no-trumps, after the simple auction 2NT – 3NT, so you know South has a whale of a hand.

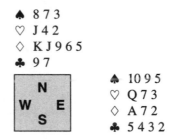

```
        ♠ 8 7 3
        ♡ J 4 2
        ◇ K J 9 6 5
        ♣ 9 7
                        ♠ 10 9 5
        N               ♡ Q 7 3
    W       E           ◇ A 7 2
        S               ♣ 5 4 3 2
```

Declarer wins your partner's opening club lead and plays the queen of diamonds on which partner plays the eight. Of course you duck – South must have at least a doubleton diamond. He continues with the four of diamonds and partner plays the three on which declarer plays dummy's jack.

Do you grab your ace now? Of course not, partner has clearly signalled his doubleton and you only need to count up to thirteen to know that declarer has another diamond and if you release your ace he will regain the lead and cross to dummy to enjoy the rest of the diamonds. However, think about what would be the right thing to do if partner had played the three of diamonds on the first round of the suit and followed with the eight of diamonds. This time you must not let dummy's jack of diamonds take the second trick. If you do, declarer will abandon the suit and is very likely to run home with nine tricks. Your partner did not peter, so he clearly holds the ten of diamonds and the job of cutting declarer off from dummy has already been accomplished.

Holding-up

Below is another example of when a defender must not thoughtlessly go up with his winners too soon. It might seem safe enough to do so when you have two stoppers in declarer's suit, but the timing of when you take these two tricks is vitally important.

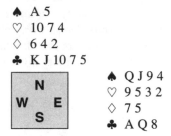

♠ A 5
♡ 10 7 4
◊ 6 4 2
♣ K J 10 7 5

♠ Q J 9 4
♡ 9 5 3 2
◊ 7 5
♣ A Q 8

Again South, who opened one spade, is playing in three no-trumps. You're sitting East and your partner leads the queen of diamonds which declarer ducks. He wins the diamond continuation with the king and leads the nine of clubs, on which West plays the two. You ponder on whether partner has three or only one, and you realise that, for the sake of the defence, it had better be three, because if declarer has four clubs there is no way in which you can stop him from making three tricks in the suit. You must duck, allowing the nine of clubs to win the first trick. When declarer, pleased that the queen of clubs appears to be on his left, leads low and finesses the ten of clubs, you win with the queen of clubs, noting that partner followed with the four of clubs, confirming he had three clubs, and declarer only two. As you can't play a diamond back to partner, you exit with the two of hearts. Let declarer try to develop his own spade suit – there's no need to try to remove the ace of spades from the table, as dummy's clubs are dead ducks! Here's the complete deal:

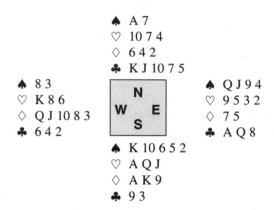

♠ A 7
♡ 10 7 4
◇ 6 4 2
♣ K J 10 7 5

♠ 8 3
♡ K 8 6
◇ Q J 10 8 3
♣ 6 4 2

♠ Q J 9 4
♡ 9 5 3 2
◇ 7 5
♣ A Q 8

♠ K 10 6 5 2
♡ A Q J
◇ A K 9
♣ 9 3

Do you see how vitally important it was for you to duck the first round of clubs? Don't fall into the trap of thinking it won't matter if you win the first round and duck the second. It's just the same as when, as declarer, you have a double stopper in the enemy suit but two controls to knock out in your suit. If you win immediately, dummy's clubs can be established, with the ace of spades as an entry. Don't worry about the risk of 'going to bed' with your ace of clubs – you can cash it when you win a spade trick later on. The next example is a little more difficult still:

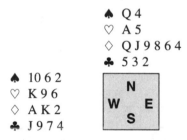

♠ Q 4
♡ A 5
◇ Q J 9 8 6 4
♣ 5 3 2

♠ 10 6 2
♡ K 9 6
◇ A K 2
♣ J 9 7 4

This time you are West, and have started off your defence to South's three no-trump contract with the four of clubs, after South opened one heart and rebid three no-trumps over North's two diamonds.

Declarer wins with the king of clubs and starts on diamonds immediately. You should duck the first diamond, and when you win the second round, your next play will depend on partner's card. If he discards, leaving declarer with a third diamond, you must lead your king of hearts! It may feel terrible to sacrifice your king like that, but it is the only card guaranteed to force out the ace of hearts, declarer's only certain entry to the diamonds, before your second diamond stop is taken from you. This is called a Merrimac Coup, and if you look at the full deal below you will see that, provided partner has as much as the king of spades, let alone the ace of spades, declarer can never make more than one diamond trick. It goes without saying that if declarer plays dummy's five of hearts on your king, you will follow with another heart, which will have the same effect:

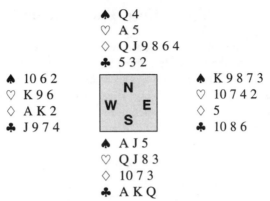

```
                    ♠ Q 4
                    ♡ A 5
                    ◇ Q J 9 8 6 4
                    ♣ 5 3 2
  ♠ 10 6 2                            ♠ K 9 8 7 3
  ♡ K 9 6          N                  ♡ 10 7 4 2
  ◇ A K 2       W     E               ◇ 5
  ♣ J 9 7 4        S                  ♣ 10 8 6
                    ♠ A J 5
                    ♡ Q J 8 3
                    ◇ 10 7 3
                    ♣ A K Q
```

If you cut declarer off from dummy's diamonds, he can't make more than eight tricks.

The last defensive duck we want to show you is a deliberate attempt to deceive declarer.

It will be enough just to show you one suit this time:

```
                    ♡ 8 2
  ♡ J 10 9 5 4                        ♡ A Q 7
                    ♡ K 6 3
```

Against South's three no-trump contract West leads the jack of hearts. East can read this as the top of a suit headed by the ♡ J-10-9, and he knows that the king of hearts must be with South. If East has next to no high cards other than his hearts, it would be right for him to go up with the ace of hearts and continue with the queen of hearts to unblock and also to drive out South's king, in the hope that partner will have an outside entry. But if East, from his count of the points in dummy, his own hand, and what declarer is known to hold from his bidding, is pretty sure that his partner won't have an outside entry, he must try to tempt declarer into thinking that West holds the ace of hearts. If East smoothly plays the queen of hearts at trick 1, what is South to do? It would take a nerve of iron to duck the queen of hearts (which would be right as the cards lie) when South fears that the lead was from something like ♡ A-J-10-5-4. Yet once he puts up the king of hearts at trick one, unless he can run for home with eight more tricks, he will go down as soon as East wins a trick and leads his ace of hearts and third heart.

Ducking to Keep Trump Control

A declarer playing in a trump contract has always to be careful to keep control of the trumps so clearly it must be of great benefit to the defenders if they can use their trump holdings to destroy declarer's control. Have a look at the following deal. You are West and against South's contract of four hearts you lead the king of diamonds. You did not choose one of your black doubletons to try for a ruff. This is rarely right when holding long trumps yourself.

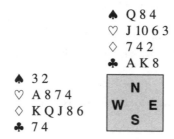

♠ Q 8 4
♡ J 10 6 3
◇ 7 4 2
♣ A K 8

♠ 3 2
♡ A 8 7 4
◇ K Q J 8 6
♣ 7 4

The king of diamonds holds the first trick so you lead another to your partner's ace and he returns a third one which declarer ruffs and leads the king of hearts which you duck, noting with pleasure that partner follows. The queen of hearts comes next and again you duck. Now declarer is fixed. If he plays a third round of trumps you will take your ace and lead a master diamond, forcing dummy to ruff. You will eventually be able to take a trick in each red suit. If declarer leaves trumps alone and plays on the black suits, you will score a ruff with your eight – and no one fails to win a trick with the trump ace!

Notice how important it was for you to keep the trump ace till the third round and then continue with diamonds. If you play the ace too early then declarer can accept the ruff and dummy's last trump will draw your last one.

The complete deal was as follows.

```
                    ♠ Q 8 4
                    ♡ J 10 6 3
                    ◇ 7 4 2
                    ♣ A K 8
     ♠ 3 2                                ♠ 10 9 7 5
     ♡ A 8 7 4          N                 ♡ 5
     ◇ K Q J 8 6    W       E             ◇ A 10 3
     ♣ 7 4              S                 ♣ 10 9 6 3 2
                    ♠ A K J 6
                    ♡ K Q 9 2
                    ◇ 9 5
                    ♣ Q J 5
```

Second Hand Plays High

So now for some thoughts, not about ducking, but about rushing up with high cards as second-in-hand, going right against the rule that says 'second player plays low'. In the defence of no-trump contracts, the general rule is that if it is your long suit which is to be established, partner must sacrifice his high cards to preserve yours as entries. If it's the other way round, then it's your duty to try to safeguard your partner's entries to his long suit.

Here again you are in the West seat.

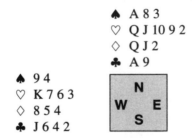

```
                    ♠ A 8 3
                    ♡ Q J 10 9 2
                    ◇ Q J 2
                    ♣ A 9
     ♠ 9 4                N
     ♡ K 7 6 3      W         E
     ◇ 8 5 4            S
     ♣ J 6 4 2
```

North has opened one heart over which your partner bid one spade and South concluded the auction by bidding three no-trumps. You lead the nine of spades. Declarer runs this round to his own hand and wins with the queen of spades, your partner encouraging with the seven. Declarer now leads a low heart. Don't sleepily play a small heart yourself, or reassure yourself by saying that second hand plays low. What can it cost you to put up the king of hearts and lead your four of spades, just in case your partner's only entry to his spades is the ace of hearts? Precisely nothing, because if the ace of hearts is in the South hand, your king could only win one trick for the defence. The thing is to take that trick when you want to, not when declarer wants you to! Here's the full deal::

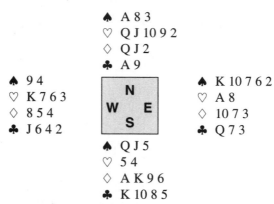

♠ A 8 3
♥ Q J 10 9 2
♦ Q J 2
♣ A 9

♠ 9 4
♥ K 7 6 3
♦ 8 5 4
♣ J 6 4 2

♠ K 10 7 6 2
♥ A 8
♦ 10 7 3
♣ Q 7 3

♠ Q J 5
♥ 5 4
♦ A K 9 6
♣ K 10 8 5

Now declarer's goose is cooked as, whatever he plays to the second round of spades, the suit is cleared for the defence when partner wins his ace of hearts, and you win three spades and two hearts.

Did you observe how vitally important it was that partner ducked with his king of spades at trick one? If he makes the mistake of going up with it and playing another spade, then it won't help for you to go up smartly with your king of hearts because you now have no spade left to continue the attack on the suit.

PART IV
GENERAL

29
Laws and Ethics

Perhaps it will surprise you that this subject is included in this book but, after all, you wouldn't embark on, say, a game of tennis without knowing at least something about the rules, and surely the same goes for bridge. We want also to dispel the idea that when you're playing a 'friendly' rubber, it's bad manners to insist on sticking to the correct rules. In tennis, if you served a double fault, you would never expect to be given the point and nor, in golf, would you dream of saying 'well, you missed the putt, but we'll count it as in'. So in bridge, a game with both laws and ethics, you should stick to the correct procedures.

The first thing you ought to know is that there are two sets of Laws, one governing rubber bridge and the other for players of duplicate bridge. At this stage in your learning it is probably mainly the Laws of Rubber Bridge which will concern you, but we'll tell you some of the most important differences between them and Duplicate Laws. We might as well also warn you that both sets of laws are pretty complicated, and that you really ought to have a copy of the Laws of Rubber Bridge so that you can look them up if something funny happens, and sort it out. However well you think you know them, always check. In tournament bridge, a director always carries a copy of the laws. By agreement between the four players some of the provisos of duplicate bridge may be observed when playing rubber as their rather stricter requirements make the game fairer.

The Opening Lead

In rubber bridge, once the auction is over, the player on declarer's left makes his chosen lead as you have always done. In duplicate bridge the player on lead lays his card face downwards on the table, and asks his partner if he has any questions about the bidding. If partner says he has no questions, the leader faces his card. This is a very good law, as it prevents a lead out of turn, as if the wrong person has tried to lead, the other three can stop him before he has shown the face of his card.

One point to remember is that if the leader's partner asks a question about the auction that makes the leader want to change his card, he may not do so. He should have asked his own questions before he chose his lead. Declarer, too, can ask for a review of the bidding, but after play has started he can't ask more than what the contract is.

Inspecting the Previous Trick

The next point concerns looking back at the previous trick. In rubber bridge, any player may inspect a trick before he or his partner has played to the next one. At duplicate, once a player has turned his own card face down, he may not ask to see the card played to that trick by any of the other three players. As long as his own card is still face upwards, he can ask for any or all of the other three to be shown to him, even if their owners have turned them face down.

Alerting

Two laws of duplicate bridge don't apply to rubber bridge at all.

The first concerns 'alerting'. The partner of a player who makes a conventional bid must make sure his opponents understand that the call is not a natural one by knocking on the table. The player whose turn it now is to bid may now ask the player who alerted (not the player who made the conventional call) for the meaning of the bid before he makes his own call. For instance, say South has opened one heart, West has passed, and North bids four clubs, South must knock the table because he knows that he and his partner are using 'Swiss' so that four clubs is conventional, and has nothing to do with the club suit. Now East, whose turn it is to call, may ask South the meaning of the four club bid. Our advice is not to ask unless you really want to know, as it is not unknown for a partnership to have got its wires crossed, and explanations aloud may help them more than you. Wait until the end of the auction.

The Stop Law

The second duplicate law that does not apply to rubber bridge is known as the 'stop' law. Any player at any stage of the auction who is about to make a bid which misses at least one level of the bidding must say the word 'stop' before he makes his bid. For example, 'stop – two clubs' or, if the opponent on his right has bid, perhaps, one spade, and he wants to jump to three hearts, he must say 'stop – three hearts', because he missed a round of bidding when he said three hearts instead of two hearts. In the same way, North in the paragraph above should have said 'stop – four clubs' as this was a jump bid as well as being conventional.

The reason for this is to allow the player whose turn it is to bid next extra time to think without making an obvious hesitation, as the jump bid may throw his thinking a little. Long pauses before a player bids or passes obviously give away that he has something to think about, so the player who follows the 'stop' bid must pause for 8–10 seconds whether he needs to or not, before bidding or passing. It is unethical to give away, by looking bored or disinterested, that there is nothing to think about.

Revokes

The law governing a revoke has now been made the same in both rubber and duplicate bridge, and is not quite so harsh. Once the revoke is established, play continues to the end of the deal. Then, if the offending side won the trick on which the revoke occurred, that trick, plus one other trick if the offenders have won one, is transferred to the non-offending side. If the offenders did not win the revoke trick, then one trick is transferred, provided the offenders actually won a trick after the revoke. If the player who revokes wins a trick with a card he could have played to the revoke trick, then the penalty is two tricks. If the offenders don't win a trick, then there's no penalty at all. After all, if they didn't gain by the revoke, why should they be penalised at all? They can, of course, keep all the tricks they won before the revoke.

Lead Out of Turn and Penalty Cards

Something which frequently causes a bit of an argument at the table is what happens when someone does succeed in making the opening lead, face up, from the wrong hand. At duplicate call the director and let him explain your choices – don't try to settle the argument yourself. At rubber bridge you won't have a director, so the players must settle the arguments. Declarer has four choices.

1   He can accept the lead from the hand on his right, dummy puts down his cards, but the next card played is from declarer's hand, not from dummy. In other words the trick is played the wrong way round.

2   He can lay down his hand as dummy and have his partner become declarer

3   Declarer can tell the player on his left to make the opening lead and order him to play a card of the same suit as the one incorrectly led, or forbid him to lead that suit at all for as long as he holds the lead. If declarer makes either of these choices then the card wrongly led is picked up.

4   He can tell the player on his left to make any lead he likes, but then the card wrongly led remains down on the table and becomes what is known as a penalty card which has to be played at the first legal opportunity.

It's worth remembering that declarer has certain rights against the partner of a player who has a penalty card.

Declarer can't have penalty cards. If he wants to, he can show every card in his hand to the defenders – it can't harm their defence, can it?

Cards can become penalty cards during play too. When either defender plays a wrong card, and this is pointed out to him, he may not pick it up and put it back into his hand. It has to stay face up on the table and be played as soon as it legally can. This can happen when, for example, a player accidentally plays two cards to the same trick. One will become a penalty card.

If a defender leads out of turn during play, the card becomes a penalty card, and the lead reverts to the player whose turn it correctly was. If declarer leads from his own hand instead of dummy, or vice versa, then he picks up the wrong lead, and plays any card he chooses from the correct hand.

The matter of penalty cards is complicated and differs between rubber and duplicate bridge. Always check with the rules and follow the procedure laid down.

Insufficient Bids and Calls out of Rotation

Things can also go wrong in the bidding! Common problems arise when insufficient bids are made and when bids or passes are made out of turn. The rules are quite complicated and too involved to summarise here – so once again keep the rule-book handy!

Dummy's Rights and Duties

If dummy is behaving properly it should never happen that declarer leads from the wrong hand or fails to follow suit. Don't ever get into the bad habit of looking at your partner's or the defender's hands when you're dummy. If you do, you forfeit all your rights, and now it's your fault if declarer does something you should have been quick enough to stop him doing.

Dummy's rights are limited, though. He mustn't do or say anything else, and he mustn't play a card from dummy, even if it's a singleton, until declarer tells him to do so.

Defender's Rights

Defenders have no rights during the play of the cards in duplicate bridge! They may not attempt to prevent one another from revoking or refer to the number of tricks won or lost during play.

In rubber bridge the defenders can ask one another about a failure to follow suit in order to prevent a revoke occurring. However, the card played in error may not be picked up and must be played at the first legal opportunity. See the full Laws for the rules regarding penalty cards, which are now quite complicated.

Ethics

Both rubber and duplicate laws lay great emphasis on the ethics and proprieties of the game. Many players, particularly of rubber bridge, are very lax about the proprieties. Here are some of the most frequent crimes that are committed – do you recognise you or your friends as being guilty of any of them?

1   Picking each card up from the table as soon as it is dealt, without waiting for the deal to be completed.

2   Saying 'a spade' instead of 'one spade' or 'pass' instead of 'no bid', or, what is worse still, sometimes using one way of speaking and sometimes another.

We remember taking over a class of near beginners a few years ago and correcting them for variously saying 'pass' and 'no bid'. We were told that everyone they played with did this, as 'pass' meant 'I have a really rotten hand' and 'no bid' meant 'I can't quite bid but I am not completely worthless either', or words to that effect! That sort of thing, whether they knew it or not, is cheating. No member of either partnership at any game of bridge must ever make a bid or a signal the meaning of which is a secret from the other pair. In duplicate bridge the players have cards with their systems written out, but playing rubber bridge either at home or in a club, players must be equally honest with the opponents. We hope no one really wants to win by cheating, for this is what it amounts to.

3   Making one's bids in different tones of voice according to whether one is happy with the bid or not. By this we mean that partner opens, say one heart for example, you bid rather slowly in a dull voice 'two hearts' or in a happy and bright tone 'three hearts'. That is definitely passing unauthorised information, as is making your bid with a rising inflection, which is as good as saying 'partner, I like this – can you bid again?'. How can partner not be influenced? All bids must be made at the same speed and in the same tone of voice.

4   Hesitating for an appreciable time before making a bid, and then passing. Everyone at the table then knows that you had something to think about, which puts a terrible strain on partner because, to be truly ethical, the partner may then bid again only if he can justify the bid on the cards he himself holds. If you were hesitating about whether or not to open the bidding, it's better in the end to open, or your partner may well be silenced. If you open, no one will know whether you were wondering whether to open on a rotten 12 points, or choosing between two alternatives to describe a strong hand. No 'unauthorised information' will have been passed across the table.

5   Drawing your partner's attention to the fact that you have a part-score or are, or are not, vulnerable, during the bidding or play of the hand.

6   Pointing out to partner that you have already taken five tricks in defence, and that declarer has 'all the way to go'. This is clearly a hint to partner to cash a winner quickly, if he has one, or to give you a ruff, or some other such action. Just keep quiet – there should be no chatting at all during the bidding or play.

7   Putting dummy down with a long explanation of why such and such a bid was or was not made.

8   Playing a card from dummy, even if it is a singleton, before declarer has told dummy to play it.

9 Reaching across, when you are declarer, and playing a card from dummy before your left-hand opponent has played his card, which you will see done time and time again. It is not only impolite and unethical, but against the rules, and defenders should take full advantage of declarer's playing out of turn. You can do this by sitting back, if it was your turn to play, and saying 'after you, partner', so that fourth player puts down his card before second player. This can be of the greatest possible help to the defence, and it certainly stops that particular declarer in his tracks if he goes down in his contract because he discourteously played out of turn! He won't do it again in a hurry.

10 Hesitating during the play when you have only a singleton you can play, which is a particularly appalling crime. It is nothing less than cheating, as it is a sharp-practice method of trying to trick your opponents into thinking that you have more than one card you could have elected to play in a particular suit.

You will appreciate that the above hints are only some of the more important and interesting points from the Laws and Proprieties of bridge. We couldn't begin to summarise them in one short lesson, but if you are really interested in playing the game correctly, you'll find it well worth while investing in a copy of either or both the codes of laws, according to which variety of bridge you play.

APPENDIX

Contract Bridge Scoring Table
Rubber Bridge

		Und'bld	D'bld
Trick points for declarer	**Odd tricks bid and won in**		
	Clubs and Diamonds each	20	40
	Hearts and Spades	30	60
	No-trumps first	40	80
	each subsequent	30	60

Redoubling doubles the doubled points. 100 trick points constitute a game.

		Not vul.	Vul.
Premium points for defenders/declarer		Value	Value
	Overtricks		
	Doubled each	100	200
	Making doubled contracts	50	50
	Making redoubled contracts	100	100
	Undertricks		
	Undoubled each	50	100
	Doubled first	100	200
	second & third	200	300
	subsequent	300	300

Redoubling doubles the doubled points for overtricks and undertricks.

Premium points for declarer/holder

Honours in one hand (declarer dummy or defenders)
4 trump honours   100
5 trump honours or 4 aces at no-trumps   150

Slams bid and won
Small   not vul 500   vul 750
Grand   not vul 1000   vul 1500

Rubber points
In two games 700   In three games 500

Unfinished rubber: Winners of one game score 300 points. If only one side has a part-score in an unfinished game it scores 100 points. Vulnerability does not afect points for honours.

Contract Bridge Scoring Table Duplicate Bridge

Bonus points:

A non-vulnerable game bid and made	300
A vulnerable game bid and made	500
A part-score bid and made	50
A doubled contract bid and made	50
A redoubled contract bid and made	100

Slam bonuses and trick values are as in rubber bridge
Honours do not count.

Slam scores

		Small				Grand	
		6	6x	6+1	6x+1	7	7x
Spades	Vul.	1430	1660	1460	1860	2210	2470
Hearts	Non.	980	1210	1010	1310	1510	1770
Diamonds	Vul.	1370	1540	1390	1740	2140	2330
Clubs	Non.	920	1090	940	1190	1440	1630
No-trumps	Vul.	1440	1680	1470	1880	2220	2490
	Non.	990	1230	1020	1330	1520	1790

Teams of Four Scoring
Scale of International Match Points

Difference on board				IMP	Difference on board				IMP
0	–	10	=	0	750	–	890	=	13
20	–	40	=	1	900	–	1090	=	14
50	–	80	=	2	1100	–	1290	=	15
90	–	120	=	3	1300	–	1490	=	16
130	–	160	=	4	1500	–	1740	=	17
170	–	210	=	5	1750	–	1990	=	18
270	–	310	=	7	2250	–	2490	=	20
320	–	360	=	9	2500	–	2990	=	21
370	–	420	=	9	3000	–	3490	=	22
430	–	490	=	10	3500	–	3990	=	23
500	–	590	=	11	4000 and over			=	24
600	–	740	=	12					

Table of Standard Leads

Holding	Against trump contracts	Against no-trump contracts	Holding	Against trump contracts	Against no-trump contracts
'Blind' leads – i.e. when partner has not bid a suit:					
A-K-J +	A	A	J 10 9 x x	J	J
A K Q x x x	A	A	10 9 8	10	10
A K Q x x	A	K	J 10 x x	x	x
A K Q x	A	K	A Q J x x	A*	Q
A K x	A	K	A Q 10 9 x	A	10
A K	K	K	A Q x x x	A	x
A K J 10	A	A	A J 10 x x	A	J
A K J x	A	K	A 10 9 x x	A	10
A K J x x	A	K	K J 10 x x	J	J
A K J x x x	A	A	K 10 9 x x	10	10
A K x x x x	A	x	Q 10 9 x x	10	10
A K 10 9 x	A	10	A x x	A	x
A K x x x	A	x	K J x	x	x
K Q J x x	K	K	K x x	x	x
K Q 10 x x	K	K	Q 10 x	x	x
K Q x x x	K	x	J x x	x	x
Q J 10 x x	Q	Q	K x x x	x	x
Q J 9 x x	Q	Q	x x x	Top then middle **	
Q J x x x	x	x	x x	Top first	

* From this point onwards, 'blind' leads from these combinations and others like them are to be avoided if defending a suit contract, unless nothing more promising can be found.

** An alternative method is Middle Up Down, which avoids any possible confusion with a lead from a doubleton, and the loss of 'tempo' for the defence in trying to give partner a ruff on the third round.

When partner has bid during the auction and you intend to lead his suit, when defending a no-trump contract, lead low from any three- or four-card holding, unless you hold two honours when you should lead one. From any doubleton lead the top card. When defending a trump contract lead the highest card you hold in partner's suit.

Index